W9-ACD-679

Willa Cather and the American Southwest

Willa Cather and the American Southwest

Edited by John N. Swift and Joseph R. Urgo

University of Nebraska Press, Lincoln and London

Financial assistance for the manuscript's preparation was provided
by the Louis and Hermione Brown Humanities Support Fund at
Occidental College.
Library of Congress Cataloging-in-Publication Data
Willa Cather and the American Southwest / edited by John N. Swift
and Joseph R. Urgo.
p. cm.
Includes bibliographical references and index.
ISBN 0-8032-4557-2 (cloth : alk. paper)
1. Cather, Willa, 1873–1947—Knowledge—Southwestern States.
2. Women and literature—Southwestern States—History—20th
century.   3. Southwestern States—In literature.   4. Landscape
in literature.
I. Swift, John N.   II. Urgo, Joseph R.
PS3505.A87 Z945 2002
813'.52–dc21
2001052242

Contents

2. THE PROFESSOR'S HOUSE
Richard H. Millington
The Experience of Meaning in *The Professor's House*, 71

Merrill Maguire Skaggs
Cather and the Father of History, 80

Tom Quirk
Twain and Cather, Once Again, 89

3. DEATH COMES FOR THE ARCHBISHOP
Mary Chinery
Willa Cather and the Santos Tradition in *Death Comes for the Archbishop*, 97

Christopher Schedler
Writing Culture: Willa Cather's Southwest, 108

Manuel Broncano
Landscapes of the Magical: Cather's and Anaya's Explorations of the Southwest, 124

Joseph R. Urgo
Multiculturalism as Nostalgia in Cather, Faulkner, and U.S. Culture, 136

David Harrell
Afterword: From *The Professor's House* to the Roundhouse—and Beyond, 150

Illustrations

Acknowledgments

The essays in this volume grew out of the Willa Cather on Mesa Verde Symposium of October 1999. We are grateful to Occidental College in Los Angeles and the Willa Cather Pioneer Memorial and Educational Foundation of Red Cloud, Nebraska, for their support in planning and publicizing the symposium. We want also to thank Judith Swain, Trudi Rose, Curtis Smart, and the entire staff of the Far View Lodge at Mesa Verde, Colorado, who in generously inventive ways provided the symposium's organizers and participants with an extraordinary experience of literature and landscape. The participants themselves—plenary speakers, paper presenters, and Cather enthusiasts and conversationalists—supplied infectious intellectual energies that led us to see this collection as not only possible but necessary. After the symposium, Cynthia Marugg of Occidental College helped to sustain the project, lending it her considerable administrative skills as it moved toward publication. Occidental's Louis and Hermione Brown Humanities Support Fund provided assistance in the last stages of the manuscript's preparation. Finally, we thank our families: Cheryl, Benjamin, and Jesse Swift, and Lesley and George Urgo—best friends and traveling companions in Cather's gorgeous Southwest and elsewhere.

Willa Cather and the American Southwest

John N. Swift and Joseph R. Urgo

Introduction

Literate Tourism and Cather's Southwest

Willa Cather was throughout her life an enthusiastic traveler, a planner of summer vacations and a visitor of tourist attractions. Her itineraries often provided the important sites for her novels and stories: London, France, New England, the American Southwest, Quebec, Virginia. Moreover, tourists themselves became critical figures in Cather's fiction. Despite her well-known use of classical motifs of displacement, exile, and migration, her characters also travel simply for pleasure. Her favorite tourists—neither natives nor immigrants, but *visitors*—move observantly through foreign places collecting impressions. They are intelligent, curious, courteous to their surroundings, and not averse to souvenirs or detours. They pursue an insistent interest in finding a significant reflection, in discovering some creative relation to a strange landscape. Cather's good tourists include (among others) Thea Kronborg in Arizona, Claude Wheeler in France, and Jean Latour in New Mexico among the pueblos and missions. She also created occasional exemplary bad tourists who were blunderingly insensitive to their surroundings, like "Marge" and "Jim," the chattering, smoking, dirty-knickered American motorists of "The Old Beauty."

Writing about Sarah Orne Jewett, Cather pitied the denatured modern New Yorker, "knowing no more about New England (or country folk anywhere) than he has caught from motor trips or observed from summer hotels" (*Not Under Forty* 93). Yet after she left Nebraska, motor trips and summer hotels were her own main means of contact with many of her settings. Like her contemporary and acquaintance D. H. Lawrence, Cather was a quick student of place; as with Lawrence, her friends always noticed the focused intensity of her curiosity, her quick impassioned connectedness to people and

places. Even on a Manhattan bus ride in 1910, Elizabeth Sergeant could see
Cather's "vigor, her authenticity, her delight in the landmarks. . . . There was
so much she did not want to see and saw not. What she did see she selected
instinctively and made it so her own that her impulsive sharing of it gave it
a sort of halo of brightness" (46). In the Southwest a few years later, Edith
Lewis described her as "intensely alive to the country—as a musician might
be alive to an orchestral composition he was hearing for the first time" (101).
On all of her holiday journeys she solicited and listened eagerly to the stories
of natives and of other tourists (her fiction is full of "chance meetings" in
hotels and on trains and boats). She visited museums and galleries, and she
read (to famous advantage) old books she picked up in hotels: among others,
Howlett's *Life of the Right Reverend Joseph P. Machebeuf* at La Fonda in
Santa Fe in 1925 and Parkman's *Count Frontenac and New France under
Louis XIV* at Quebec's Chateau Frontenac in 1928.

Cather's special talent as a tourist—the source of the "halo of brightness"
that pervades her narrated landscapes—was an ability to *read* her worlds,
articulated through story and history, as meaningful texts, framed, annotated,
and vivified by an immense literary record of human striving. Landscape and
high culture (usually European) were inseparable. In *My Ántonia*—to give
a small example—the muddy prairie beyond Jim Burden's rooming-house
window is illuminated by an evening star hanging "like a lamp suspended by
silver chains—like the lamp engraved upon the title-page of old Latin texts,
which is always appearing in new heavens, and waking new desires in men"
(298). Such a vivid "textualizing" habit left its traces everywhere in Cather's
work, inextricably entwining writing and scenery, converting a world of inert
things to readable text and assimilating it to the great glittering continuum of
human ideas.

From its first appearance as a romantically impossible destination in her 1909
short story "The Enchanted Bluff," the American Southwest had a special
fascination for Cather as a writer. It also posed a special challenge to Cather
the tourist because it resisted her habit of cultural assimilation. To her friends
she described her first encounter with its big strangeness and vacancy—a 1912
visit of several weeks to her brother Douglass in Flagstaff, Arizona—through
fearful images of human smallness, of (in Sergeant's words) "hanging on by
one's fingertips, measuring oneself with that ancient image, Death, which
so easily overpowered a white man in this environment" (123). Her later
vision in *Death Comes for the Archbishop* of the desert as incomplete and

unassembled, a "country . . . still waiting to be made into a landscape" (95), echoes Jim Burden's anxiety upon arriving on a Nebraska prairie that was "not a country at all, but the material out of which countries are made" (*My Ántonia* 8). In 1912 she summoned her literary resources to "read" the desert and recalled an impressively austere image from Balzac of human absence: "Dans le desert, voyez-vous, il y a tout et n'y rien; Dieu sans les hommes" ("In the desert, you see, there is everything and nothing; God without men") (Woodress 11). It is not surprising that she was grateful to return to the conventional civilities of upper-middle-class New York.

But in Arizona, in response to the land's oppressive vacancy, she had begun a project of textualizing and humanizing the Southwest: finding art and culture in Walnut Canyon's cliff dwellings; learning missionary and Indian legends from the Flagstaff priest; and falling in love with her Mexican "Antinous," the beautiful singer Julio, who allowed her to imagine a high Aztec civilization that might rival that of the classical Europe that she loved, and from which she drew his nickname. This difficult project, sustained through four more visits to the Southwest and memorialized directly in three novels, energized Cather's career. Struggling to find human significance in a gorgeously indifferent and apparently sterile landscape, she began to articulate a set of metaphors for cultivating the wild that informed all of her work after 1912 and culminated in *Death Comes for the Archbishop* and Jean Latour's restored garden: a triumph of familiarization simultaneously literal and allegorical.

Although all of Cather's encounters with the Southwest involved her in the double modes of humanizing suggested by her 1912 attraction to Julio/"Antinous"—importing and imposing an ordering European tradition while "discovering" a mirroring indigenous American one—her August 1915 visit to Mesa Verde, Colorado, dramatically clarified these oppositions. The trip replaced an ambitiously planned tour of wartime Germany with S. S. McClure and Isabelle McClung, a tour derailed by the strong objections of McClung's father. Instead, Cather took Edith Lewis west, choosing the remote young national park at Mesa Verde and its famous cliff dwellings (under excavation by the Smithsonian) as their holiday destination. At Mesa Verde she found (at least in imagination) not scattered cryptic remains, the shards of culture that sometimes surface in the American soil, but whole cities in stone: the tangible, complex architecture of a nobly humane past, replete with technology, science, art, religion. In Cather's 1925 dramatization of this discovery in *The Professor's House*, her archaeologist-priest Father Duchene speaks words of cultural reassurance to Tom Outland: "Your tribe," he says, "were a superior people. . . . [I]n an orderly and secure life they developed considerably the arts of peace" (219). Their pottery is identical to that of lost Crete. By the end of his stay on the mesa, the Virgil-reading Tom has so thoroughly annotated and assimilated its landscape to classical high culture that

> when I look into the *Aeneid* now, I can always see two pictures: the one on the page, and another behind that: blue and purple rocks and yellow-green piñons with flat tops, little clustered houses clinging together for protection, a rude tower rising in their midst, rising strong, with calmness and courage—behind it a dark grotto, in its depths a crystal spring. (252–53)

Such a mingling of place and text is literate tourism at its most ambitious and audacious. Not yet itself wholly allegorical, it prefigures Cather's victorious allegories of *Death Comes for the Archbishop* and *Shadows on the Rock*.

The essays in this volume are themselves very literal attempts at "literate tourism," the results of a self-conscious experiment in the relationship between language, culture, and place. Cather's liking for recreational travel and the centrality of visited landscapes in her fiction have combined since her death to create a kind of sacred itinerary for her readers: Red Cloud, Grand Manan Island, Avignon, Aix-les-Bains, Santa Fe, Quebec, the Shenandoah Valley. More than with most writers, Cather readers and scholars have become tourists themselves. Since the early 1970s they have met periodically in these places (at least the North American ones) and in her "home" cities, Pittsburgh and New York, to share reevaluations of her work.

In late October 1999, under the auspices of Occidental College and the Willa Cather Pioneer Memorial and Educational Foundation, a group of about one hundred gathered at Mesa Verde—more accessible than in 1915, but for most still a long way from familiar landscapes. For three days the visitors stayed at the Far View Lodge on the mesa top, simultaneously conducting a conventional academic meeting and unabashedly collecting impressions and mementos in the cliff dwellings, along the canyon rims among the piñons, in the National Park Service's museum, and in the lodge's stores. From its inception, the symposium organizers intended to use tourism—the transient, curious relationship of the individual to the significant land—as a paradigmatic structure for reunderstanding Willa Cather's complicated relationship to the American Southwest.

Collected in this volume are some of the best papers from the Mesa Verde

Symposium. Part 1, "On Mesa Verde," centers on what we might call Cather's aesthetics of the Blue Mesa (perhaps translated so because "Green Mesa" in English is as disconsonant as "Mesa Azul" is in Spanish). The essays in Part 2, *The Professor's House*," focus more generally on the novel that contains Cather's most extended use of the mesa. Part 3 moves beyond Mesa Verde to the Southwest region, bringing us to *Death Comes for the Archbishop*, Cather's novel of missions, cultures, and historical change.

We begin at the heart of the matter, with Mother Eve, the wrapped figure at the center of "Tom Outland's story," as the center of *The Professor's House*. John N. Swift argues that we need this figure "to be something other than what she is," something beyond her literal existence as the "dried human body" discovered by Tom in the Eagle's Nest. This need of ours, which is addressed throughout the novel and embodied by the dried figure, signals a cultural system of representation designed to signify and envelop *female* in ways that serve masculine interests. And from this wrapping the coverage begins: Tom wraps and names Mother Eve; St. Peter edits and projects Tom; Cather places the narratives in juxtaposition; Swift comments, interprets, unwraps. Nonetheless, by "Unwrapping the Mummy" clothed by Tom, Swift accuses himself of rewrapping her in the language of critical self-consciousness, thus setting the stage, in this collection, for a series of raps at Cather's Mesa Verde aesthetics.

The first of these involves a closer look at Mother Eve's people. In "Anasazi Cannibalism: Eating Eden," Ann Fisher-Wirth reviews current anthropological scholarship which suggests that Anasazi civilization practiced cannibalism—a theory that has given rise to considerable debate between anthropologists and the descendants of southwestern native cultures. Fisher-Wirth links this controversy to one more familiar to readers of *The Professor's House*: that of Cather's use of anti-Semitism in her creation of Louis Marsellus, St. Peter's Jewish son-in-law. Between Anasazi cannibalism and the interpretive challenges posed by Marsellus, Fisher-Wirth identifies a representational crisis in our tendency to idealize peoples about whom we know very little and in our predicament of reading through the varied lenses of history. Cather neither knew the theory of Anasazi cannibalism nor, in 1925 when she published *The Professor's House*, could she have known how the twentieth century would come to scrutinize anti-Semitic representation as a matter of survival. Fisher-Wirth examines parallel discomforts as successively idealized Edens are consumed by evolutions in readerly perspectives.

Cather scholars have come to expect that her narrative details are well worth a thorough investigation. Not at all coincidental or arbitrary, according to Matthias Schubnell, is the role played by the German collector, Fechtig, who purchases Anasazi curios from Roddy Blake and ships them home for sale to German museums. "From Mesa Verde to Germany: The Appropriation of Indian Artifacts as Part of Willa Cather's Cultural Critique in *The Professor's House*" provides an important historical context for Fechtig's role in the novel. The Berlin Museum, for example, sponsored forty-eight expeditions to gather Indian artifacts between 1881 and 1901, an era in which German anthropology exerted strong influence in the United States, including on the organization and arrangement of museum collections. Tom's nationalist fervor in the face of Roddy's sale ("they weren't mine to sell—nor yours! They belonged to this country, to the state, and to all the people") resonates with greater significance in the light of the novel's setting in an era when ethnology expanded our understanding of nationalism to include prior inhabitation of lands transformed by cultural expansion. Cather thus participates in expectations of her time that American art find value and draw on traditions considered native to its soil.

Marilee Lindemann continues a materialist examination of nationalism in "Fear of a Queer Mesa?: Faith, Friendship, and National Sexuality in 'Tom Outland's Story,'" a study of "Cather's entanglement in processes of national self-imaging and her fascination with the semiotics of American bodies and physical spaces." Identifying the Blue Mesa as a "queer" space, Lindemann sees it as a site on which bodies, families, and nations are radically interrogated and creatively reimagined. The historical context for Cather's cultural intervention is the presidency of Theodore Roosevelt, with its (and his) concerns for the virility of American national identity. Citing Roosevelt's numerous claims for the morally and physically "strenuous life," Lindemann finds Tom wholly responsive to Roosevelt's ideological constructions of masculinity. The most transformative information Tom brings to Cliff City from Washington DC is not the Smithsonian's lack of interest in Anasazi artifacts but rather intolerance for the queer lifestyle he had lived on the mesa with Roddy. Tom would rather go to war, where he undergoes a culturally sanctioned, nationally significant death in Flanders.

John J. Murphy turns our attention away from the material setting of *The Professor's House* toward its status, in his view, as a marker in Cather's own religious journey. In "Holy Cities, Poor Savages, and the Science Culture: Positioning *The Professor's House*," he suggests that Cather's two Anasazi-inspired novels, *The Professor's House* and *The Song of the Lark*, can be read in the context of her travels to France and in the context of her career as a whole. Finding scholarly concerns with Cather's Southwest inspiration important but perhaps too literal, Murphy charts Cather's spiritual development in "forty-five years of fiction-writing rising from and returning to Medieval European culture via excursions to the American Southwest and Northeast." Cather's own spiritual journey reverses the journey taken by so many of her migratory characters—she moved east, not west, toward the Christianity embodied in European cathedrals, toward Henry Adams's sense of the Virgin's power in human affairs. Cather traced the alternative to modernism she sensed in the ruins of southwestern paganism not to American nationalism but to Judeo-Christian spirituality. In *Death Comes for the Archbishop*, when Cather returns to Anasazi history in the American Southwest, it was not to revisit its ruins but to project thoughts about God and Christianity across its landscape, just as she would later do across the landscape of Quebec in *Shadows on the Rock*. Murphy's sophisticated interpretation of Cather's aesthetic purposes haunts the enterprise of this collection, cautioning us against easy conceptualizations based on what we think is evidence.

Such haunting continues in Richard H. Millington's "The Experience of Meaning in *The Professor's House*," the first of a series of essays in part 2 that attempt to get inside the novel's structure(s). Millington finds the generative spirit of the novel less in any "overarching or undergirding, romantic or religious, structure" than in the free-floating juxtapositions that arise from a text steeped at once in an intense domesticity and an equally intensive transcendence of domestic space. The "fresh air that blew off the Blue Mesa" (Cather, *On Writing* 31–32) also blows homeward: life in Cliff City for Tom, while bearing the signs of an authenticity that counters domestic triviality, becomes a matter of household goods and the selling of our stuff. "Tom Outland's Story" is no window onto an alternative to what ails Professor St. Peter; on the contrary, it is a mirror, signaling both fullness and emptiness, which, "for all the apparatus of authenticity" Cather invokes for Tom's experience, may reflect the surrounding pattern of St. Peter's life as well as Cather's sense that the domestic is among the more powerful forces in human life—more consequential, more revealing, and more meaningful than what we consider the larger historical and cultural movements that define us.

"One fact that, like a disreputable neighbor, we have seen but not known for decades is that Willa Cather was friendly with Mark Twain." So Merrill M. Skaggs begins an essay that uncovers Twain and Cather in conversation. In "Cather and the Father of History," Skaggs presents evidence of a friendship based on mutual interests and fueled by a series of exchanges embedded in literary allusions—references by Twain to Red Cloud and unmistakable traces of Twain in the characterization of Godfrey St. Peter's consciousness. There may have been a valentine from the old lion to the young cub, and there is certainly a line of succession between the two writers that compels us to think again about the traditions into which Cather sought to insert her aesthetic vision. Tom Quirk was not at the Mesa Verde conference, but we asked, based on his own speculation concerning Twain and Cather, what he thought of Skaggs's theory. In "Twain and Cather, Once Again" he finds that Skaggs's evidence helps explain the processes and interactions that led Cather to think of herself as a western writer within the American literary landscape, far from the Jamesian drawing rooms of New York City and European longings.

What emerges clearly in these essays is that Cather's connections to the American Southwest are intertwined with a range of biographical, cultural, and historical influences. Part 3 leaves Mesa Verde and, using *Death Comes for the Archbishop* as its central text, examines the influence of the larger region, a space of intersecting cultures and histories. Mary Chinery provides vital historical information in "Willa Cather and the Santos Tradition in *Death Comes for the Archbishop*." The santos tradition—flat pictures painted on cottonwood, called *retablos*, and three-dimensional carved figures, called *bultos*—predates the arrival of the Jesuits (and continues to evolve) as an embodiment of the confluence of Indian and Hispanic civilizations. Cather knew this tradition—perhaps through Mabel Dodge Luhan, who collected santos artifacts—and integrated it into *Death Comes for the Archbishop*. Jean Latour's attitude toward the tradition, his acceptance of some of it, and his nervousness about it reflect general Catholic, as well as modern, responses to folk art rooted in pre-Christian spirituality. As Luhan's collection exemplifies, there was a kind of "modernist mania" for santos in the era of the novel's composition, making Cather's text itself reflective of the mesmerism that folk culture exerts on the modernist imagination.

Christopher Schedler expands on Cather's employment of a range of cultural influences in "Writing Culture: Willa Cather's Southwest," focusing in particular on the interaction of cultures in the American Southwest. Schedler considers the development of Cather's cross-cultural aesthetic in *The Song of the Lark*, *The Professor's House*, and *Death Comes for the Archbishop*, a process whereby Cather moves from simple cultural evolutionism to an exploration of the nature of borderlands and cultural dialogism, anticipating more recent critiques associated with modern anthropology. He observes that Cather, anticipating in *Death Comes for the Archbishop* "the dialogic approach to culture of contemporary anthropology," balances the logic of difference and the logic of equivalence . . . allowing for an examination of the discursive processes through which 'others' are represented." In her later fiction, Cather's understanding of culture moved away from an earlier dependence on racial essentialism and thus contributed in important ways to the progress of the twentieth century in comprehending human difference. Cather's intellectual growth, moreover, was signaled by the growing sophistication of her aesthetics, marked also by a representation of cultural variety dependent less on comparison than on dialogical processes of exchange.

In juxtaposing Cather with Rudolfo Anaya, Manuel Broncano, in "Landscapes of the Magical: Cather's and Anaya's Explorations of the Southwest," places Cather in the tradition of pan-American magical realism. Broncano locates a series of parallels between Anaya's *Bless Me, Ultima* (1972) and *Death Comes for the Archbishop*, picking Cather up, in a sense, where Schedler left her, as a major contributor to contemporary conceptualizations of borderlands. Although the novels "differ radically on the surface," Broncano's analysis shows them sharing deep, vital concerns for preserving remembrance, incorporating the magical, and negotiating borders "between country and pueblo, the white and the mestizo, the rational and the uncanny (or miraculous), Christ and the primeval gods of the Indians, the desert and the farm." Such negotiations lead both novels to the employment of the grotesque, a method closely associated with magical realism in both its Anglo-American and Latin American forms. Broncano's study is groundbreaking for its claim that the topography of the American Southwest compels a kind of parallel response by Cather and Anaya, despite their obvious differences, so that as we move beyond matters of plot and representation, we find kindred spirits across generational, cultural, racial, and ideological divides.

Finally, Joseph R. Urgo completes the volume's attempt to move Cather into contemporary cultural discourse in "Multiculturalism as Nostalgia in Cather, Faulkner, and U.S. Culture." Urgo juxtaposes two major figures in twentieth-century literary representation, Faulkner's Isaac McCaslin, from *Go Down, Moses*, and Cather's Archbishop, Jean Latour. "The two men lead very different lives but each wrestles with the fundamental American dilemma of how to contemplate difference." In the end, Urgo finds that such contemplation leads to a fundamentally American form of *indifference*, where cultural variety produces a kind of ennui, as long as such differences do not interfere with modes of production and corporate capitalism. Cather's moves toward multicultural understanding anticipate the century's move in that direction, as does her sense that multiculturalism is infused with a nostalgia for lost races, for forgotten nativity, and for the idea that cultural difference makes a difference. Cather's multicultural novel, *Death Comes for the Archbishop*, emerges, in these last three essays, as a landmark in twentieth-century American intellectual history, providing grounds for analysis and debate of issues that remain central to contemporary visions of the nation's future as a multiracial, multiethnic society.

David Harrell's seminal book *From Mesa Verde to* The Professor's House (1992) established for scholarship the importance of the Southwest to Cather's imagination and was in many ways the Mesa Verde symposium's foundational text. No longer a professional critic, Harrell recounts the ways in which Cather's vision has accompanied his personal journey out of the academy and into a career in public service, making the point "that one need not be an artist or an academician to recognize or participate in the creative impulse that Cather recognized as the design of life." Harrell's afterword closes the volume.

1. ON MESA VERDE

John N. Swift

Unwrapping the Mummy

Cather's Mother Eve and the Business of Desire

Some of this essay originates in my unsettling encounter in 1998 with one of the possible sources for Cather's "Mother Eve": the leathery, desiccated body of a small, dark-haired Andean woman who crouches quietly behind locked doors in a white, airtight cabinet on the fourth floor of Nebraska Hall at the University of Nebraska in Lincoln. Her head tilts slightly to one side, and at first she appears dejected, her empty eyes staring downward, her mouth open slightly. She, a man (presumed to be her husband), and three children were curiosities given to the university in 1892 by the U.S. minister to Chile, and the young Willa Cather evidently saw them soon after their arrival that year (Swift and Tschetter 14). The museum's curator estimates them to be about a thousand years old. Taken off public display at some time in the twentieth century, they receive few visitors, and unlike other human remains collected in the great predations of nineteenth-century anthropological archaeology, they have no inheritors or claimants and evoke no political or national scandal. Sequestered thus outside history's main currents, opaque and self-contained in mute privacy, the woman is still intensely and disturbingly human. To open her door is to acknowledge with surprised intimacy her nakedness, her femaleness, and her deadness—and to recognize painfully that some profound violation has occurred, although its exact nature is not clear. The echoes of the encounter persisted uneasily for me and have lent some emotional urgency to the thoughts that follow concerning *The Professor's House* and its enigmatic "mummy," Mother Eve.

I have usually thought of and read *The Professor's House* like Cather's other great novels of the 1920s, as an expression of her participation in a pervasive modernist cultural/political fantasy of loss, nostalgia, and ambiguous redemption. In its typical narrative, alienated heroes confronted the diminished present in the afterglow of a strong but irrevocably lost past. This paradigm structured in various well-known ways the nostalgic fictions of Cather's American contemporaries Fitzgerald, Hemingway, and Faulkner, among others. From my own fairly straightforwardly Freudian perspective (which identifies in a culture's dreams the unspoken yearnings of a small boy, and vice versa), it is an essentially *masculine* fantasy, Oedipal or pre-Oedipal, wherein the weakened present is always haunted by gigantic parental *imagos*, at once fearful and desirable.

Seen through such an interpretive lens (even without the colorful mythology of psychoanalysis), and with irresistible encouragement from her biblically charged name, Mother Eve tends to assume for her readers any number of weighty symbolic costumes: as the spiritual ur-mother suggested by her name (Harrell, *From Mesa Verde*, 135–37); as a sometimes fearsome reminder of matriarchal power (Schwind 75ff.); as a general figure of irretrievable maternal wholeness (Swift 305); or as a type of female authorial creativity (Lindemann 110–11). In all of these guises we may catch glimpses of Cather's historical mother, Mary Virginia Cather ("Jennie," like the mule who plunges with Mother Eve to the bottom of Black Canyon), ambivalently refashioned, recovered, and lost again in her daughter's masculinized imagination. To discover Mother Eve inevitably seems to involve clothing her in significant and desirous allegory.

"Clothing Mother Eve" with meaning is a necessary activity for the characters of "Tom Outland's Story" as well as for Cather's readers. I want to continue by exploring exactly this phenomenon: Mother Eve's openness to—indeed, her demand for—interpretation. In a text self-consciously studded with "meaningful" elements, she functions as an ostentatious central hermeneutic lure or bait. I suspect, and will argue, that her presence and description arouse a particular *kind* of interpretive need, one generated in the novel's exploration of a cultural politics of gender and possession. Like Tom, Roddy, Henry, and Father Duchene, we readers of Mother Eve badly need her to be something other than what she is: speechless, self-contained, and wholly indifferent—and thus threatening—to the symbolic orderings of the men who seek to understand and possess her.

As my last sentence suggests, the argument that follows owes much to the work of the French psychoanalyst Luce Irigaray. In particular, I am influenced by her provocative speculation (in her critique of Freud's efforts to define femininity) that masculine formulations of femininity are founded in a panicky unconscious denial of difference, negativity, and, ultimately, death. Irigaray's thinking is famously and simultaneously technical and diffuse. I will note here only that she identifies Freud's fable of a small girl's self-recognition as a "castrated" (and thus deficient) boy as a critical move in culture's construction of a totalizing worldview in which the masculine is the normative and "meaning" and "value" are expressed in a dialectic of presence and absence, of the plenitude and lack of masculine characteristics and authority. Moreover, Irigaray concludes that really to *see* woman, to consider her autonomously—as something other than an insufficient or defective version of man—would mean nothing less than, in her words, "the ultimate destruction, the splintering, the break in [man's] systems of 'presence,' of 're-presentation,'" thus threatening man's entire "process of production, reproduction, mastery, and profitability" (50). Drastic as this sounds, I believe it has something to do with the radical discomfort that Mother Eve inspires, and with our need to keep her covered.

It is useful to begin looking at Mother Eve by considering what she is *not*. Despite Tom Outland's occasional use of the term, she is not, strictly speaking, a "mummy," embalmed and wrapped against destroying time, but rather "a dried human body, a woman" (Cather, *Professor's House* 191). In fact, this erroneous labeling is instructive, the first of many stories woven about her. It deserves some further attention, since it lodges her firmly in a well-known discourse to which she is nonetheless a foreigner: that of the shrouded Egyptians who caught the American public's imagination in the late nineteenth and early twentieth centuries. Cather knew and wrote of these mummies; she had seen them in the British Museum and romanticized them herself in *Alexander's Bridge*. Their defining characteristic was their wrapping; in *My Ántonia* she described the dead Mr. Shimerda's head "bandaged in white muslin, like a mummy's" (132). She wrote *The Professor's House* in the aftermath of the great Tutankhamen fever of 1922 and 1923. (It seems unlikely that Cather actually heard any of Howard Carter's famous popular lectures on Tutankhamen's tomb, since she was visiting her family in Nebraska when he passed through New York in the spring of 1923. Nonetheless, with her long-standing interest in antiquity, she could not have failed to be affected by this powerful cultural romance.) When Henry Atkins joins Tom and Roddy, he explicitly links their adventure to his youthful "ambition to go to Egypt and see the tombs of the Pharaohs" (183).

The mummy of popular culture—in some ways Mother Eve's stark oppo-

site, as we shall see—holds double fascination for us, as it did for Cather's generation. Its extraordinary encryption (hidden down tunnels in secret chambers
and nested sarcophagi beneath layer upon layer of winding cloth) suggests
value, conjuring fantastic El Doradoan treasures from a lost age of opulence—
Howard Carter's "wonderful things" glimpsed by candlelight. At the same
time, it captures the imagination because of its contradictory representations
of life and death. As a fantasy-representation (Boris Karloff's famous performance in *The Mummy* seven years after *The Professor's House*'s publication,
for instance), it embodies, simultaneously horrifically and consolingly, an
impossibly sustained, indestructible sexual desire: through technology and
necromancy, the mummy is the lover who can—and does—wait forever. Its
horror lies in the greedy inexorability of its desire, as well as in its tendency to
confuse its objects (one remembers Lon Chaney, Karloff's film successor of
the 1940s, untidily swathed in bandages, lurching slowly but unstoppably after
unfortunate young men or women resembling long-dead enemies and lovers).
Its consolation is its triumphant denial of death, its childish insistence on
passion's irresistible integrity; even in death, the mummy is a potent presence.
This kind of mummy, presumably, has some relation to the British Museum's
"priestess-mummy" invoked by Bartley Alexander and Hilda Burgoyne as
they play out their ephemeral affair in *Alexander's Bridge* (94–95).

For *The Professor's House* and the figure of Mother Eve, Cather imagined
something very different. In Tom's narrative:

> At last we came upon one of the original inhabitants—not a skeleton,
> but a dried human body, a woman. She was not in the Cliff City; we
> found her in a little group of houses stuck up in a high arch we called
> the Eagle's Nest. She was lying on a yucca mat, partly covered with
> rags, and she had dried into a mummy in that water-drinking air. We
> thought she had been murdered; there was a great wound in her side,
> the ribs stuck out through the dried flesh. Her mouth was open as if
> she were screaming, and her face, through all those years, had kept a
> look of terrible agony. Part of the nose was gone, but she had plenty of
> teeth, not one missing, and a great deal of coarse black hair. Her teeth
> were even and white, and so little worn that we thought she must have
> been a young woman. (191–92)

She appears to the adventurers as a confusing collection of negations, ab-
sences, and unanswered questions: *not* a skeleton, *not* in the Cliff City (for
Tom the mesa's cultural center), unburied and solitary (unlike the funeral
group found later), "partly covered with rags," part of her nose missing, a

gaping hole in her side. Nothing about her is immediately either particularly threatening or reassuring to Tom or the reader. Moreover, despite Henry's portentous naming and Father Duchene's later efforts to give her a sexual history, she seems wholly outside of and unconcerned with familiar structures of religion, maternal origin, or erotic desire. In short, Mother Eve initially resists (and thus solicits) interpretation through formal instability and negation: the material body is clearly and even ostentatiously present, but where one looks to understand her, one finds instead a vacancy, or at best a fragment.

I'm particularly interested in her partial covering, since it clearly distinguishes her from the overwrapped, overdressed mummies I've discussed whose essence is *the outside*, the covering or sheath: the pyramid, the funeral chamber, the ornamental sarcophagus, the coffin, the preserved body finally invisible in its fabric cocoon. Mother Eve, by contrast, lies naked and simple to the eye, her only distinction her sex—"a dried human body, a woman"—on an exposed mat in a high place. And as such, as Irigaray might say, she implicitly resists and challenges the symbolic practices of a culture that deploys a system of coverings and ornamentation simultaneously to occlude *biological* sexual difference and to subdue it to something of recognizable exchange value: a regularizing system which, in short, assigns to women the function of literally bearing value as commodities in a masculine economy (114–17).

My reading so far may seem strained, abstract and overly theorized. But we should consider here that clothing women—and clothing them for a place in a man's world—is a concern whose effects develop in interesting ways, not only in Cather's personal costuming history but also throughout her work. We should particularly recall the dead Indian woman plundered by Ray Kennedy in *The Song of the Lark* who

> was preserved as perfect as any mummy that ever came out of the pyramids. She had a big string of turquoises around her neck, and she was wrapped in a fox-fur cloak, lined with yellow feathers that must have come off wild canaries. . . . The fellow that claimed it sold it to a Boston man for a hundred and fifty dollars. (148)

(Ray gives one of the turquoises to Thea, and promises more looting and more "keepsakes" as part of his strange courtship.)

Closer at hand, we should take note in *The Professor's House* of Cather's ambivalent detailed description of precisely a "masculine economy" in operation: an economy where Mrs. Bixby's wine-stained skirt may threaten her little husband's career; where Louie overdresses Rosamond to define his social and economic station in Hamilton; where Kathleen must seek St.

Peter's help in choosing her furs; and where Lillian chides St. Peter for the modesty that prevents him from expressing open pleasure "with his wife or his house or his success" (37). St. Peter's shopping expedition to Chicago with Rosamond—"Napoleon looting the Italian palaces"—requires a look at the complicated relations of gender, costuming, consumption, and ownership; he gives up his planned purchase of a new coat for himself, overspending instead on Rosamond, "permit[ting] myself a little extravagance to be of service to the women of my family. Any other arrangement is humiliating" (135). With remarkable frequency, *The Professor's House* returns to the relations of covering, gender, and value, and it is not surprising that Godfrey St. Peter shares his most significant space with a dressmaker and her forms—or that Willa Cather, celebrating her novel's commercial success, wrote to a friend in early 1926 (aware, I like to think, of the teeming ironies of her words) "that the professor had bought her a mink coat, the first valuable thing she ever had owned" (Woodress 379).

Nor is it surprising that when an undeniably unwrapped female figure is found at the center of a novel whose overt thematic concerns (nation, knowledge, origin, ownership, inheritance) are uniformly and even overwhelmingly masculine, her finders respond immediately by covering her up, in literal cloth and with a useful symbolic history: "Henry named her Mother Eve, and we called her that. We put her in a blanket and let her down with great care, and kept her in a chamber in the Cliff City" (192). A process of normalizing Mother Eve, of inserting her into a known and interpretable symbolic discourse, conventional and Judeo-Christian, begins here. For help in elucidating this strange presence on the mesa, Tom and Roddy turn to the expert Father Duchene (whose professional title and knowledge of Virgil surely credential him as an interpreter/historian for patriarchy), and he reweaves Mother Eve into a narrative of masculine power and feminine lack, finds her a husband, and re-covers her "wound" as the punitive mark of the male:

> "I seem to smell," he said slyly, "a personal tragedy. Perhaps when the tribe went down to the summer camp, our lady was sick and would not go. Perhaps her husband thought it worth while to return unannounced from the farms some night, and found her in improper company. The young man may have escaped. In primitive society the husband is allowed to punish an unfaithful wife with death." (201)

Looked at honestly, isn't there some powerful need, something even verging on panic, that drives this weird storytelling? But isn't Father Duchene's tale, on the other hand, simply an elaborate version of giving the body the name of Eve, the primal feminine betrayer? Isn't it just additional "covering up," a paradoxical way of "making her decent" for masculine consumption (paradoxical because the only tolerable woman is the woman wounded, marked for and by her betrayal)? And in fact this entire series of gestures, from the simple blanket to the whole embroidery of adultery, is a necessary precursor to Roddy's eventual sale of Mother Eve, now a well-defined cultural commodity in a wooden sarcophagus, to the German Fechtig.

Where does Cather herself stand in all of this? Is she a critic of the masculine economy, the trading in femininity? Or is she its product and purveyor? As is typical in her work, we cannot tell; the multiple ironies of (for example) Father Duchene's speculative archaeology make any single perspective untenable. (In *From Mesa Verde*, David Harrell has summarized various interpretive positions on this passage [135]; at issue is whether we are to read Father Duchene as a voice of historical authority, as suggested by his Virgilian associations, or as a prurient fantasist, as suggested by his "slyness" and the host of qualifiers that surround his story—or both at once.) And unresolvable ironies like these structure the novel as a whole.

I will suggest, though, that in creating Tom and his story, Cather momentarily assumed, consciously or unconsciously, a voice that tried to speak from a symbolic register beyond that governed by gender and its valorizations. Unlike Ray Kennedy, Louie Marsellus, or even Godfrey St. Peter, Tom has no particular interest in "dressing up" women, literally or allegorically. His narrative openly repudiates the whole system of ornamentation and representation by which man assigns value to woman and imposes dominion on his sexual and material world: "We thought it rather contemptible," he says of the "Indian boys [who] sometimes went to a trader's with their wives and bought shawls or calico" (210). He is equally disdainful of Washington DC, the "terrible question of what Mrs. Bixby should wear" (210), and the careerist vanities of the bureaucrats who "seemed to me like people in slavery, who ought to be free" (211). And, of course, Tom plays little part in the transformation of Mother Eve, her "mummification" and commodification. Although here as everywhere else multiple ironies abound, I'm inclined to take literally Tom's famous cry to Roddy, understanding it as a pained repudiation of what I've called the "masculine economy": "I'd as soon have sold my own grandmother as Mother Eve—I'd have sold any living woman first" (221).

Tom comes finally, strangely, to *resemble* Mother Eve. Functionally, he is a dead, wordless presence at the center of someone else's narrative. Despite the various symbolic values attached to his name and memory by the novel's other characters (as "virtual" bridegroom and son-in-law, as source of inheritance, as Louie and Rosamond's house), he confers no meanings himself, attaches no exchange value to objects or people, and owns nothing himself. "Fellows like Outland," thinks St. Peter, "don't carry much luggage" (103), literal or symbolic. And like Mother Eve, who "escapes" her mummification and commodification by falling back irretrievably into Black Canyon, Tom, too, falls away from the representational economy that suffocates St. Peter, who after Tom's death recalls his fine hand:

> A hand like that, had he lived, must have been put to other uses. His fellow scientists, his wife, the town and State, would have required many duties of it. It would have had to write thousands of useless letters, frame thousands of false excuses. It would have had to "manage" a great deal of money, to be the instrument of a woman who would grow always more exacting. He had escaped all that. (236–37)

Isn't there here a longing to be free, not of desire itself, but of the *business* of desire, of the system of denials and substitutions that stitches sexuality, ownership, and commerce so grimly and tightly together?

I will conclude these speculations by briefly recapitulating my argument and by pointing to one further claim that Mother Eve and Tom make on their readers. I have suggested, somewhat fragmentarily, that in creating Mother Eve— a startlingly un-mummylike mummy—Cather offered a challenge to a cultural system of representation that denies the sexual autonomy of woman and envelops her instead in a complicated web of symbolization, all relating her to specifically masculine needs: as a defective or "weaker" man, as an unreliable object of desire, as a valuable ornament or commodity. This symbolic web is pictorialized throughout *The Professor's House* as a generalized concern with dressing the female body. Furthermore, I have tentatively proposed that Tom's story itself may be read as a kind of narrative equivalent of the image of Mother Eve. His is a strange, paradoxical voice from outside, yet one that comments on the register of gender, signification, and power: "If commodities could speak" (as Irigaray says, quoting and paraphrasing Marx), "they might possibly give an opinion about their price, about whether they consider their status just, or about the dealings of their owners" (118). They might sound a bit like Tom.

But commodities cannot speak—or, perhaps more accurately, their speech could only reinforce their subjection, and itself become commodity. Tom's narrative comes to be precisely because St. Peter plans somewhat reluctantly in his bachelor summer (his well-dressed wife and daughters finally consigned to Louie Marsellus's care) "to edit and annotate [Tom's diary] for publication" (150). In other words, we encounter "Tom Outland's Story" in the moment his speech is subjected to a framing, value-conferring public academic discourse, a *wrapping* and preserving in the conventionally known fabric of introductions and notes. And in this covering Tom will become St. Peter's valuable "intellectual property," with an erotic charge that will at last justify and explain Lillian's old jealousy—and the property of a long, talky lineage of scholars, interpreters, and critics whose end point is perhaps us. Better, perhaps, Mother Eve's way: to exist mutely and to disappear without heirs, without legacy, without a trace.

These last reflections lead me, a little uncomfortably, to my own complicity in the normalizing interpretive project whose purpose is to make sense of the different, and thus to tame and possess it. They remind me forcibly of the voyeuristic brutality—archaeological, literary, and sexual—that converts a private human into a desirable public object, a collectible, a plundered body on display, behind glass, like the family of "mummies" with whom I began this essay. Finally, these thoughts have recalled to me also Cather's own insistent autonomy as a writer and her fierce privacy—a privacy that literally outlived her in her determination to leave behind nothing of a personal self for public consumption. Mother Eve's silence may at the end speak to us after all, as Cather's rebuke or admonition to her posterity, repudiating our interpretations and attempts at possession, and demanding instead only that we respect her solitary, unfathomable passion.

Ann Fisher-Wirth

Anasazi Cannibalism

Eating Eden

> *Then everything includes itself in power,*
> *Power into will, will into appetite,*
> *And appetite, an universal wolf,*
> *So doubly seconded with will and power,*
> *Must make perforce an universal prey,*
> *And last eat up itself.–Shakespeare,* Troilus and Cressida, *I, iii*

In November 1998, Douglas Preston published an article in the *New Yorker* reviewing *Man Corn*, Christy Turner II and Jacqueline A. Turner's massive archaeological study of all the twentieth-century site evidence for the existence of Anasazi cannibalism. Preston's article was the impetus for this essay, in which I intended to focus solely on the Turners' work and its possible implications for a reading of "Tom Outland's Story" in Willa Cather's *The Professor's House.* But as I began to write, what appeared to be an utterly unrelated topic kept pushing its way to the forefront of my consciousness. Try as I might, I could not begin with anything but Louie Marsellus, Godfrey St. Peter's son-in-law. The process of writing, for me, has been to discover what Louie Marsellus might have to do with Anasazi cannibalism—what a wealthy Jewish businessman often read as antithetical to Tom Outland, the novel's golden boy and the discoverer of Blue Mesa, might have to do with Christy Turner's controversial claims regarding occurrences of nonreligious, nonritual cannibalism that took place particularly during the Chaco period, between A.D. 900 and 1300, among the Anasazi (413). My essay is in three sections: the first is on Louie Marsellus; the second is on the Turners' *Man Corn*; and the final section attempts not only to arrive at a sense of why Louie

Marsellus and *Man Corn* are linked in my mind but also briefly to probe the fraught relationship between idealization and what Laurence Buell has called "the environmental imagination."

I have always thought of Louie Marsellus, Professor St. Peter's wealthy Jewish son-in-law in Cather's *The Professor's House,* as the novel's dark horse. It is true that for the first half of the novel Cather presents him with a version of the anti-Semitism that characterizes so much modernist writing. He is a "mackerel-tinted" (43) materialist who makes a fortune capitalizing on the commercial possibilities of Tom's discovery: a gas (or, alternately, engine) that revolutionizes aviation and to which he has gained access by marrying Rosamond St. Peter, Tom's heir and "virtual widow" (45). An uxorious sensualist, he is given to rubbing cheeks with Rosamond at family dinners and proclaiming in front of his needier in-laws, "We're going to France for the summer . . . and drink Burgundy, Burgundy, Burgundy!" (108). His is the "vulgar tongue" (62)—the discourse of capital—into which, when Rosamond offers her father a stipend, he tells her he refuses to let his relationship with Tom be translated. And his is the nose. "Semitic," it "[takes] the lead" and grows "out of his face with masterful strength, well-rooted, like a vigorous oak-tree growing out of a hill-side" (43).

But during the course of the novel, Louie gradually surpasses the categories that contain him. He is the catalyst for others' greed and for others' envy; proximity to him causes both Rosamond and her mother to change "bewilderingly in some respects," and to harden, and the more arrogance takes hold in Rosamond's spirit, the more envy takes holds in her sister Kathleen's. But as St. Peter realizes, "Louie, who [has] done the damage, [has] not damaged himself." In fact, it is Louie to whom "one [appeals] . . . for the bruised feelings of people less fortunate" (161). Irrepressibly acquisitive, he is also irrepressibly generous, and though one cannot count on Rosamond to honor "the fine, the almost imaginary obligations" (63) attendant upon fortune, one can count on Louie, Cather implies, to help bail out the seamstress Augusta when she loses her investment and to make financial provisions for Tom's chief professor, the dying physicist Robert Crane. His more remarkable generosity, however, is emotional. "Visibly shaken" (168) when Rosamond tells him that Scott, his brother-in-law, has blackballed him from the Arts and Letters Club, he responds with poise and kindness both to his bitchy wife and to St. Peter, who "apologizes" to Louis "for the behaviour of his family" (169). "Oh, *that's* all right, sir," Louie replies: "As for Scott, I can understand. He was the first son of the family, and he was the whole thing. Then I came along, a stranger, and carried off Rosie, and this patent began to pay so well—it's enough to make any man jealous, and he a Scotchman!"

His remarks to St. Peter about Rosamond are even more surprising. "As for Rosamond," he says, "you mustn't give that a thought. I love her when she's naughty. She's a bit unreasonable sometimes, but I'm always hoping for a period of utter, of fantastic unreasonableness, which will be the beginning of a great happiness for us all" (170). In a novel characterized by rejections, disappointments, and denials, Louie's is the spirit of affirmation. He is joyfully flawed, exuberantly postlapsarian; and if it is apt that he is the one to capitalize on—to *materialize*—the ethereal discovery referred to at one point as the "Outland vacuum" (40), it is apt as well that in the novel's final pages he is the one to materialize the "fantastic unreasonableness" of eros and fertility: to beget new life upon Rosamond, the beautiful, cantankerous rose of the world.

For this reason, I cannot fully agree with Walter Benn Michaels's argument in *Our America: Nativism, Modernism, and Pluralism* about Cather's treatment of Louie. If, as I believe, Cather's conception of Louie alters over the course of the novel, he cannot quite bear the weight of the cultural project Michaels assigns him, whereby as a Jew he is simply an interloper and threat to the "discourse of purity" with which American modernist writers—and indeed the country itself—attempted during the 1920s to answer the question, "So what is an American?" (50, 15). On the morning of the Arts and Letters blackballing fiasco, Louie comes to pick up St. Peter from his shabby attic study and notices Tom's purple serape, which St. Peter keeps like a holy relic. Throwing it across his chest, he calls it "a very proper dressing-gown . . . for Louie" (166). I read this gesture with complete ambivalence. On the one hand, it makes Louie seem a usurper, the lesser heir to Tom's rarefied legacy; I partly agree with Michaels when he maintains that Louie "is born a citizen but remains 'foreign,'" links *The Professor's House* with *A Lost Lady* in their shared concern with purity and corruption, and sees "the Jewish Louie Marsellus" as a substitution "two years later . . . for the merely unscrupulous Ivy Peters" (47, 46). Yet as Louie stands there "throwing back the blanket with a wide gesture," he speaks lovingly of Tom not as a rival but as an "adored and gifted brother" (166), and perhaps this assumption of familial connection may be read as something other than pushiness. As St. Peter later tells Louie, his emotional generosity makes him "magnanimous and magnificent" (170).

The novel soon turns to "Tom Outland's Story," and then in book 3 to the

Professor's rediscovery of "the original, unmodified Godfrey St. Peter" (263), Tom's analogue and spiritual kin. What Louie represents is never more than a countercurrent, largely bypassed by the novel. "Infandum, regina, jubes reno-vare dolorem" (113): "You ask me, O queen, to renew an unspeakable grief"— this line from the *Aeneid*, recited by Tom the first day he appears in St. Peter's garden, casts its long shadow over nearly every dimension of *The Professor's House*. The epigram in *Finnegans Wake*, "First we feel, then we fail, then we fall," describes the inimitable trajectory of nearly every action in both St. Peter's and Tom's stories. The world and love grow old; the artifacts are sold. *The Professor's House* is imbued with what Julia Kristeva calls in *Black Sun* "an abyss of sorrow, a noncommunicable grief" (180). At its heart, as suggested by "the bust" (17), Cather's mordant trope of the non-nurturing dressmaker's dummy, the "noncommunicable grief" is melancholia, which, according to Freud, stems from "the impossible mourning for the maternal object" (184)— a mourning mostly forgotten in the dazzle of experience, but inseparable from life itself. Kristeva comments that any specific loss, "some setback or other in [one's] love life or [one's] profession, some sorrow or bereavement," can easily trigger this despair; and, of course, moving to a new house, completing his histories, thinking of Tom, and sparring with his family all help to trigger St. Peter's. Increasingly, he is living what Kristeva describes as

> a life that is unlivable, heavy with daily sorrows, tears held back or shed, a total despair, scorching at times, then wan and empty. In short, a devitalized existence that, although occasionally fired by the effort I make to prolong it, is ready at any moment for a plunge into death."
> (180–81)

The novel does not gainsay his experience; when he wins through at the end, it is only to a life "without delight" (282), to stoic patience. But, however briefly, Louie presents a counter to St. Peter's despair, as well as an alternative to Tom's solitary, essentially ascetic idealism: the alternative of worldliness and eros, which is always suspect and flawed but can be also noble. In Cather's perhaps unconscious revaluation of Louie, *The Professor's House* teaches itself one way to go forward.

Since the nineteenth-century discoveries of the ruined cities and cliff dwell-ings that Cather commemorates as Blue Mesa in *The Professor's House*, a standard view has generally prevailed in which the lost Anasazi (a Navajo word meaning "ancient enemy") were "peaceful farmers," members of a nearly utopian society which, from the tenth to twelfth centuries in Chaco

Canyon, "attained astonishing results in engineering, architecture, and art" until around A.D. 1150, when "a vast collapse apparently occurred, and Chaco, along with some of the outlying sites, was apparently abandoned" (Preston 76). But in 1967, as Preston has reported in the *New Yorker,* "a young physical anthropologist named Christy Turner II began looking at the Anasazi in a new light." While doing some research at the Museum of Northern Arizona, Turner stumbled upon a box of remains collected by Alan P. Olson at Polacca Wash on the Hopi Indian Reservation and realized that the "more than a thousand human bone shards" looked "exactly like *food* trash" (68). In 1969 he presented a paper cowritten with Nancy Morris titled "A Massacre at Hopi," which argued that

> the bones belonged to a group of thirty people—mostly women and children—who had been "killed, crudely dismembered, violently mutilated," and that the heads, in particular, showed extreme trauma. . . . "[E]very skull, regardless of age or sex, had the brain exposed." Heads had been placed on flat rocks and smashed open, apparently so the brain could be removed. . . . [M]ost of the bones—not only the skulls— also showed marks of cutting, chopping, dismembering, butchering, "defleshing," and roasting. (78)

The paper went on to argue that the bones dated from the late 1600s, the result of a massacre at Awatovi, a Hopi village, that happened because the chief of Awatovi asked five Hopi villages to band together and purge his village from the "spiritual stain" (Preston 78) of witchcraft and conversion to Christianity. The Awatovi men were killed, and the women and children were seized as captives, but, apparently, an argument broke out between tribes carrying away the women and children, and the captives were murdered at a place since known as Mas-teo'-mo, the Death Mound. Hopi legends of the attack survive. Nevertheless, as Preston writes,

> To suggest that the Hopi could have deliberately tortured, murdered, mutilated, cooked, and eaten a defenseless group of women and children from their own tribe seemed to make a mockery of a hundred years of . . . scholarship. The paper was looked upon with deep skepticism by many of Turner's peers, and the Hopi objected to what they considered a crude slur on their ancestors. (79)

Undaunted, during the next thirty years Turner and his wife and colleague, Jacqueline, continued to study the archaeological record for signs of cannibalism, going all the way back to the Hopis' ancestors, the Anasazi. An enormous volume published in spring 1998 called *Man Corn: Cannibalism and Violence in the Prehistoric American Southwest* is the detailed and, I believe, convincing account of their discoveries—one of the chief ones being that claims for the existence of prehistoric southwestern cannibalism are nothing new. Numerous archaeologists have published such claims since 1902 (Turner 5), but, as Preston puts it, "the profession, perhaps blinded by the conventional wisdom, had ignored the reports, the notes, the evidence, the very bones" (79).

"Taphonomy" is "the study of postmortem bone distribution and mod-ification" (Turner 6); it explains how an assemblage of bones is deposited and damaged after death. "Perimortem" refers to "the variably brief phase at or around the time of death" (Turner 10–11). In order to arrive at a hypothesis of cannibalism, the Turners required "a minimal taphonomic signature consisting of . . . six key perimortem damage features . . . in human bones from a charnel deposit: (1) breakage, (2) cut marks, (3) anvil abrasions, (4) burning, (5) many missing vertebrae, and (6) pot-polishing" (24)—the last of which refers to the tiny scratches found at the ends of bones when they are stirred in a cooking pot. Reviewing the archaeological findings in 76 claims for southwestern cannibalism or violence, and in 42 cases personally examining the human remains, the Turners concluded: "At least 38 Southwest episodes of cannibalism took place that involved the eating of at least 286 persons of all ages and both sexes" (413). Of these, 243 occurred during the Pueblo II–III period, between A.D. 900 and 1300 (408–9), when the Chaco civilization was at its height. Particularly interesting is Turner's suggestion that Richard Wetherill's "broad experience and two discoveries of extraordinary prehistoric violence"—at "Cave 7" in Utah and Snider's Well in Colorado, both in 1893—may have led him to influence archaeologist George H. Pepper in thinking "about cannibalism as the cause of broken and burned bones" (60) when Wetherill worked with Pepper several years later at Pueblo Bonito and Peñasco Blanco.

No actual claim has been made that cannibalism took place at Mesa Verde. However, Turner mentions the following three things as ongoing mysteries concerning violence at Mesa Verde. The first is the mummy Wetherill found in Ruin 16, north of Long House at Mesa Verde. In *The Professor's House,* Tom comes upon the mummified body of a woman whom Father Duchene, the priest assisting Tom, calls Mother Eve, and for whom Father Duchene hypothesizes a story of sexual transgression. But the actual mummy is the body of a man—not a woman like Mother Eve—who, as Gustaf Nordenskiöld theorized, may have "fallen in defence of his hearth and home" (qtd. in Turner

66). The second is the body C. F. Merbs discovered, with its head apparently twisted off. And the third is eight human hair specimens microscopically examined, screened from human feces (67). Though at this time human skeletal research is not permitted on collections in Mesa Verde National Park, Turner's comment seems apt: "A systematic reexamination of the Long House skeletal remains along taphonomic lines would be useful" (67).

But claims for the existence of Anasazi cannibalism are far less controversial than Christy Turner's theories as to its causes. He believes that when the Toltec empire collapsed and its capital, Tula, fell around 1170, "vanquished warrior-cultists" may have migrated northward with their complex of beliefs involving human sacrifice and cannibalism (463). Various forms of evidence—artifacts, feathers, turquoise, and so forth—have long suggested that Mesoamericans came north; recently, Turner has discovered what he believes to be a new sort of evidence "in the form of deliberately modified teeth" (471). However, several theories besides cannibalism or social terror have been put forward to explain the abandonment of the cliff dwellings, including a prolonged drought, overpopulation resulting from the protected nature of the cliff dwellings and their spatial limitations, and soil exhaustion on mesa farmlands.

Nevertheless, according to Turner, there is compelling evidence that Toltec thugs may have introduced cannibalism into the Chaco area as a form of social control, until eventually, "terrorizing the local populace into submission . . . veered into social pathology" (463) and the culture collapsed in a reign of terror. This would explain both the "near-extinction of the entire prehistoric Southwest population" (qtd. in Preston 88) and the subsequent retreat into inaccessible cliff dwellings and mesas. "A people who had the hardihood to build there," Tom says of the Anasazi at Cow Canyon, "who lived day after day looking down upon such grandeur, who came and went by those hazardous trails, must have been, as we often told each other, a fine people. But what had become of them? What catastrophe had overwhelmed them? (213). Christy Turner suggests the answer: what overwhelmed them was the "ancient enemy"—themselves, the Anasazi.

Finally, what might Anasazi cannibalism have to do with Louie Marsellus, and how might becoming aware of Anasazi cannibalism change one's reading of *The Professor's House*? At the heart of *The Professor's House*, Walter Benn Michaels argues, is a concern with racial and cultural purity played out in the opposition between Rosamond St. Peter's two lovers—Tom, whose "ancestors" (242) are the Anasazi, the native Americans, and Louie Marsellus, the "exotic," the Jew (78; see Michaels, *Our America* 47). Though I believe Michaels badly oversimplifies Cather's depiction of Louie, he is right to perceive the novel's obsession with purity. At the heart of *The Professor's House* is a concern with nearly every imaginable form of purity, as well as the loss or corruption of purity: "first we feel, then we fail, then we fall." Ethereal states—whether the "toujours plus naif" of blue Lake Michigan, the "very much in love" between Godfrey and Lillian, the Outland "gas," or the "consuming light" of Tom's months alone on Blue Mesa—*inevitably* decline. The only way off the mountain is down, as Tom descends Blue Mesa, as inspiration gives way to materialization.

For years I read *The Professor's House* with tremendous nostalgia, seduced by its dream of perfection, of "silence and stillness and repose—immortal repose," of a village that "sat looking down into the canyon with the calmness of eternity" (201). My research into Anasazi cannibalism has not destroyed the beauty of that vision, but it has made me intensely aware of the contingency of that vision. And there's something else as well. I realize that, like many others who focus on environmental issues, I have idealized people about whom I actually knew very little. I have unquestioningly embraced what Shepard Krech calls "the ecological Indian"—the myth of Native Americans as intrinsically and universally possessing "the secret of how to live in harmony with Mother Earth, to use what she offers without hurting her" (Hughes, qtd. in Krech 22)—in a desperate desire for something to hold against what I hate: a culture so ravenously materialistic, so obsessed with capital, that it is destroying the very grounds of our existence. To consider the possibility of Anasazi cannibalism, social chaos, and rule by terror does not compromise my awareness that no culture has ever been as environmentally destructive, on as large a scale, as our own, or my desire to discover and realistically assess more ecologically responsive and responsible forms of life.

Cather had little chance of knowing about Anasazi cannibalism. Therefore, its discovery does not so much make problematic her idealization of Blue Mesa as it makes problematic our response to that idealization. For me, the de-idealization that results from its discovery has led back to Louie Marsellus, who is himself, of course, far from ideal. His behavior as a developer, amassing a fortune by capitalizing on the possibilities of an "Outland engine" that is "revolutionizing" wartime aviation (40), is nothing to emulate; Louie is intimately involved with the processes that have by now led to global depredation. A prosperous businessman, he has an eye to the main chance; his generosity is the flip side of his greed. Often read as little more than a complacent

Jewish bourgeois about whom Cather's feelings neither change nor develop during the course of the novel, Louie opens Cather to the charge of anti-Semitic stereotyping pure and simple. But perhaps the usual discomfort with Cather's creation of Louie resembles the similar discomfort with studies that revise the idea of the "ecological Indian"; the complexity of real situations, real people who inhabit each category—"the Jew," "the Native American"—is sometimes overlooked, marginalized by a combination of the reader's guilt and the reader's idealism. And what interests me about Louie is that unlike Tom, unlike St. Peter—indeed, unlike myself in earlier readings of *The Professor's House*—he is no idealizer. Louie has neither Eden nor the dream of Eden; he is paralyzed neither by melancholia nor by its lesser form, nostalgia. In the metaphor of my title, he has eaten Eden. In the metaphor of Rosamond's name, his love not just for her, but for the Rose which is the world, makes him exuberantly, lovingly postlapsarian. And it seems to me that the choices that would sustain our flawed, passionate, barely still-salvageable life on earth will at last begin only once Eden is eaten and we know that it has been eaten.

Matthias Schubnell

From Mesa Verde to Germany

The Appropriation of Indian Artifacts as Part of
Willa Cather's Cultural Critique in *The Professor's House*

In "Tom Outland's Story," Willa Cather establishes a connection between
Mesa Verde and Germany through the cliff-dweller artifacts Tom Outland and
Roddy Blake collect and that Roddy sells to the German curio dealer, Fechtig,
who exports the objects. This seemingly minor detail in *The Professor's House*
raises three questions that this essay seeks to answer. First, is there a factual
context that would make Fechtig's activities plausible—that is, did German
collectors play a significant role in the appropriation of Indian art, and did
German anthropologists and museums concern themselves with American
prehistoric remains? Second, is there a direct link, as the novel suggests,
between the objects the Wetherills found at Mesa Verde and a German
collection? And third, how does this connection to Germany fit into Cather's
cultural critique in *The Professor's House*? The exploration of these issues
also sheds light on how Cather manipulates the historic material to suit her
novelistic ends.

Upon returning from Washington after his failed attempt to interest the
Smithsonian in the discovery of Blue Mesa, Tom learns from Bill Hook that
Roddy had "got a lot of money for [his] stuff" (214). "I begged him to tell me
what stuff he meant. 'Why, your curios. This German, Fechtig, come along;
he'd been buying up a lot of Indian things out here, and he bought your whole
outfit and paid four thousand dollars down for it'" (214). Hook explains to
the bewildered Tom that

> Fechtig took the stuff right along with him, chartered a freight car, and
> travelled in the car with it. I reckon it's on the water by now. He took
> it straight through into Old Mexico, and was to load it on a French
> boat. Seems he was afraid of having trouble getting curiosities out of

the United States ports. You know you can take anything out of the City
of Mexico. (215)

Outraged and in disbelief, Tom hurries to Blue Mesa and confronts Roddy:
But I never thought of selling them, because they weren't mine to
sell—nor yours! They belonged to this country, to the State, and to
all the people. They belonged to boys like you and me, that have no
other ancestors to inherit from. You've gone and sold them to a country
that's got plenty of relics of its own. You've gone and sold your country's
secrets, like Dreyfus. (219)

This quarrel spells the end of the men's friendship, but it is important to note
that there is no resentment against the German collector in Cather's portrayal
of Fechtig. He acts like a gentleman to the locals, takes great care in preparing
the artifacts for shipping, and even travels in the same car with them to ensure
their safe journey to Europe. Not even the irate Tom condemns the German.
One reason for this may be Cather's tacit approval of Fechtig's fondness for
the artifacts. The name "Fechtig" resists direct translation. While the word
per se does not exist in German, it resembles an adjectival form of "fechten"
or "Gefecht"—the first meaning "fencing" or "fighting," the second meaning
"battle"—suggesting that the German is engaged in the highly competitive
race among European museums and private collectors to secure Native
American artifacts. Cather creates here and in her disparaging description
of the Smithsonian's lack of concern for Indian artifacts the impression that
America lags behind Europe in the appreciation for the First Americans'
cultural productions, a claim that is not supported by the facts and which will
be discussed in more detail below.

Fechtig, of course, is not the only German in Cather's work who is drawn
to Indian artifacts. In *The Song of the Lark*, Fred Ottenberg's ranch hand,
Henry Biltmer, becomes Thea Kronborg's guide to Panther Canyon. Biltmer
"had gathered up a whole chestful of Cliff-Dweller relics which he meant to
take back to Germany with him some day" (278). So what are we to make
of Cather's association of German characters with the remnants of Native
American cultures? A look at the history of German collections of American
Indian artifacts shows that Cather's portrayal of Germany's keen interest in
Native American art is indeed accurate.

According to Walter Krickeberg, the appearance of the earliest examples of
Indian ethnographica in Germany dates to the second half of the eighteenth
century, a result of Germany's relatively late participation in the colonization
of America. The first, often undocumented Indian artifacts found their way

to Germany in the wake of the military involvement of soldiers from Hesse and Braunschweig in the American Revolutionary War (4). Ethnology as a distinct field of study emerged in the first half of the nineteenth century. Among its founders were Henry R. Schoolcraft, George Catlin, and German explorer Prinz Maximilian von Wied, who, accompanied by Swiss painter Karl Bodmer, traveled up the Missouri from St. Louis to the Yellowstone between 1832 and 1834. On this journey they gathered a wealth of information about Native tribes, many of which were decimated shortly afterward, in 1837, by a devastating smallpox epidemic. Along the way, Wied collected Indian artifacts that were later purchased by museums in Berlin, Stuttgart, and Rome (Krickeberg 8). Krickeberg ranks Wied's monumental work *Travel to the Interior of North America, 1832–34*, published between 1839 and 1841, as the defining study in ethnology of its time.

Between 1850 and 1855, numerous other German scholars and artists visited Indian tribes, among them Edwin Thompson Denig, head of the American Fur Company at Fort Union; Balduin Moellhauser, the illustrator who accompanied Duke Friedrich Wilhelm Paul of Württemberg on his third American journey along the Platte and Upper Missouri Rivers; and Johann Georg Kohl, who corroborated Schoolcraft's studies in the Great Lakes area (Krickeberg 5). Their works gave impetus to ethnographic study and raised interest in American Indian cultures in Germany.

The precursor to the Berlin Museum of Ethnology was the ethnographic collection that grew out of the Royal Prussian Art Foundation, directed by Leopold K. W. A. von Ledebur from 1839 to 1873. During his tenure, he strove to secure the best available collections of North American Indian artifacts for the Berlin Museum (Krickeberg 9). As early as 1824, the Prussian Art Foundation acquired the collection of Captain Hadlock. In 1829 and 1834, objects imported by the Prussian trading vessel Princess Louise from the Aleutian Islands and the American Northwest coast increased the holdings (Krieger and Koch 221). In 1840 the Prussian Consul Hebenstreit purchased forty-four valuable objects from the Comanches in Texas (Krickeberg 9). In 1844, thirty-eight pieces from the collection of Maximilian zu Wied were acquired for 121 Taler, representing the Mandan, Hidatsa, Grosventre, and Blackfeet cultures (Krickeberg 10). Numerous other collections were added in the 1860s and 1870s.

In order to fulfill its mission to build a world-class ethnographic collection, the Berlin Museum supported forty-eight expeditions between 1881 and 1901. Of major importance was the collaboration with the Norwegian Capt. J.

Adrian Jacobsen who supplied nearly seven thousand objects he had collected on his journey to the American Northwest coast and Alaska between 1881 and 1883. On the final leg of his journey, Jacobsen traveled to Arizona before returning to Berlin (Krieger and Koch 223–24). It is uncertain how many pieces from the American Southwest he furnished to the museum. It is, however, clear that the Southwest became a central focus of the museum's activities at the turn of the century. In 1901 the Keam collection added to the museum's holdings 2,502 pieces of Hopi artifacts, the Friedmann collection 172 pieces from New Mexico, and the Voth collection another 77 objects from the Hopi (Krieger and Koch 228).

A good example of how seriously and discriminately the Berlin Museum collected Indian ethnographica is its consideration of George Catlin's work. In 1855, George Catlin sold 10 oil paintings and 104 ink drawings to Friedrich Wilhelm IV. When he offered the Berlin Museum of Ethnology an additional collection of drawings in 1870, Adolph Bastian, founder and first director of the institution, rejected the purchase because he considered Catlin's depictions of Native people's physical features as too vague and inconsistent to provide any ethnographical information (Krickeberg 6). (George Catlin, of course, also encountered great obstacles in the United States in getting his work accepted and exhibited. His generally futile efforts to do so lend some credence to Cather's claim that America was not greatly interested in a record of Native American cultures. For a very detailed study of Catlin's ordeal, see Dipple.) The Berlin Museum's decision was in line with its general philosophy, articulated as early as the 1830s by Karl Graf Bruehl, to seek objects of great scientific importance as opposed to those of merely aesthetic appeal. Bastian himself insisted that the museum's mission required the collection of original, unadulterated objects in order to achieve a comprehensive representation of aboriginal life (Krieger and Koch 3). He deemed the establishment and preservation of a near complete collection of artifacts as his generation's duty:

> A period like ours which destroys with an iron hand numerous aboriginal tribes and ploughs up the earth in every direction owes it to future generations to preserve as much of the information that remains from humanity's childhood and youth as is necessary to understand the development of the human spirit. What is now being destroyed is irretrievably lost to posterity. (qtd. in Krieger and Koch 3–4)

It is important to note here that this mission statement is based on the same assumption as the vanishing race theory that motivated people like George

Catlin, Edward Sheriff Curtis, and many others to preserve a record of Indian cultures considered to be on the verge of extinction.

Important additions to the collections in Berlin were made throughout the second half of the nineteenth century and up until 1925, by which time exceptional examples of Indian art had become so scarce they hardly ever came up for sale. These purchases were made in a climate of stiff competition for Native American artifacts among European institutions and collectors. A good example is Gustaf Nordenskiöld's collection of Mesa Verde artifacts which he shipped to Sweden and which now resides in the National Museum in Helsinki, Finland (Reader's Digest 67). The extensive collections of Indian artifacts in Berlin, Stuttgart, and Frankfurt are evidence that Germany competed successfully in the race to secure for posterity representative examples of North American Indian material culture.

That Germany was indeed a plausible destination for the Mesa Verde objects is further supported by the direct influence German scholars exerted on the budding science of anthropology in the United States and on the way in which the Smithsonian Institution organized and arranged its collections, reflecting Germany's advanced knowledge in the study of prehistoric artifacts. Charles Rau, a graduate of the University of Heidelberg, arrived in New Orleans in 1848 and later became the chief archaeological collaborator to Joseph Henry, the first secretary of the Smithsonian Institution (Hinsley 42). Rau applied his expertise "in the typographical, descriptive classifications of Old World prehistory" (Hinsley 44) to the newly discovered archaeological finds in America.

Otis T. Mason, the first curator of ethnology in the National Museum (1884–1908), also drew heavily on German ideas in museum management: "In 1873 Mason introduced culture history to Washington. Mason's principles of museum classification derived directly from the system of Gustav Klemm at the Museum of Ethnology in Leipzig" (Hinsley 84; 87–88). Both Klemm and Mason sought to establish centralized collections to facilitate comparative study, argued for the study of "a single, continuous historical growth" in human development from savagery to enlightenment, and incorporated cutting-edge natural science into their cultural studies, asserting that "Nature is the foundation of culture" (Hinsley 88). In 1889 Mason embarked on a tour of European museums that brought him into contact with two leading German scholars: Adolph Bastian, head of the Berlin Museum of Ethnology, and Adolphe B. Meyer, director of the Dresden Museum of Zoology and

Anthropology. He shared with them ideas on ethnographic exhibit techniques and acknowledged the intellectual significance of their encounters by saying, "I ought to have taken this trip thirty years ago. My intellectual life has been in a bag" (qtd. in Hinsley 109).

This brief account of German influences on American ethnology in the nineteenth century would not be complete without the mention of Franz Boas, a German émigré whose anthropology department at Clark University in Worcester, Massachusetts, granted the first Ph.D. in anthropology in 1892. In 1899 he developed "the first comprehensive anthropology program in the United States" (Rothman 14). Boas began a dialogue with Otis T. Mason following the latter's 1886 Eskimo exhibit at the National Museum, arguing that "the Museum's strongly developmental arrangement severely hampered study" (Hinsley 98). Instead of comparing similar phenomena among different peoples, Boas proposed to study them in their specific social and historical contexts. His claim that "civilization is not something absolute, but that it is relative, and that our ideas and conceptions are true only so far as our civilization goes" (qtd. in Hinsley 99) became the central tenet of his theory of cultural relativism.

This summary of the German involvement in the collecting of Native American artifacts and of the influence of German anthropological scholarship on American ethnologists and museums provides a context that helps to explain why Cather may have chosen the German Fechtig as the collector who appropriated the Mesa Verde artifacts as raw material for ethnographic study in Germany.

To answer the more specific question of whether any of the Mesa Verde objects actually found their way to Germany, one must consider a tantalizing clue in one of David Harrell's notes that identifies Berlin as the possible destination of Fechtig's collection:

> The Wetherills may also have suggested the nationality of Cather's foreign buyer of artifacts. Jesse Nusbaum, superintendent at Mesa Verde during the twenties, thirties, and forties, quotes John Wetherill as saying that part of one of their collections "was purchased by a German [unnamed] who sent it to a museum in Berlin." (Jesse Nusbaum to Don Watson, 8 Dec. 1948, Mesa Verde Research Center, Mesa Verde National Park, Colorado) (234n68)

Walter Krickeberg's detailed study titled *Older Ethnographica from North America in the Berlin Museum for Ethnology* contains nothing to support Jesse Nusbaum's or John Wetherill's assertions. My correspondence with

Hans-Ulrich Sanner at the Berliner Museum für Völkerkunde, however, led to a surprising discovery that verifies John Wetherill's statement: according to Sanner, Eduard Seler, director of the American collections of the Berlin Museum of Ethnology, purchased 264 artifacts from Richard Wetherill at the St. Louis World's Fair in 1904. Seler wrote this about his purchase:

At the World's Fair in St. Louis, I purchased a collection of baskets, sandals, and pottery by the cliff-dwellers and basketmakers of the cave dwellings in the canyons of southern Utah, compiled by Richard Wetherill (who also acted at the time on behalf of Gustav Njordenskiöld and the Hyde-Clark Expedition), for the sum of $500.00. (Museum für Völkerkunde, Erwerbungsakte vol. 26, Akte 511/05)

Given that the collection mentioned in Seler's letter originated in Utah, Cather's connection between Mesa Verde and a German collector is fictitious, but the document supports both Cather's link between the Wetherills and Germany and her broader claim that Germany's interest in the material cultures of North American tribes resulted in the acquisition of numerous important collections. It is worth noting that Eduard Seler also bought a small collection of Pima baskets and some examples of Zuni and Casas Grande pottery from Richard Wetherill's archrival, J. W. Benham, who operated a stall next to Wetherill's at the World's Fair (Sanner).

It remains to be shown how Cather's choice of nationality for the buyer of the Mesa Verde artifacts relates to her novel's broader intentions of critiquing American culture. The novel attacks a number of areas in American life, including widespread conspicuous consumption, declining educational standards, dehumanizing urban development, and a cultural bureaucracy enamored with European art. This said, why would Cather choose a German collector to purchase and export the precious Anasazi objects? Obviously, her intent was to suggest that America lacked the sophistication to appreciate the earliest examples of American art, while Europeans were eager to appropriate them.

She must have felt so intent on creating the impression that America's foremost ethnological institution, and by implication America as a whole, disregarded the value of Native American artifacts that she did not let facts get in her way. This is the more surprising since it was a group of Smithsonian archaeologists that rescued Cather and Edith Lewis when they lost their way at Mesa Verde in 1915 (Woodress 264). As Harrell has pointed out in considerable detail, Cather's depiction of the Smithsonian Institution as an organization indifferent to Native American art and artifacts is unjustified. (For a detailed study of the relationship between the Wetherills and the Smithsonian and the institution's efforts to support archaeological expeditions, the study of Indian languages, and the publication of scholarly works on Native American cultures, see Harrell's *From Mesa Verde to* The Professor's House and "'We Contacted Smithsonian': The Wetherills at Mesa Verde.") It is true that in the early years of the Smithsonian, Joseph Henry, the institution's first secretary, argued against the establishment of a museum because he feared that maintaining it and caring for large collections would be beyond the means of Smithsonian's bequest. He was opposed to seeking government funding for a museum because of "his desire to keep Smithsonian science independent from political influence" (Hinsley 66). Consequently, the Smithsonian did not support the collecting of anthropological specimens before the Civil War. Between 1867 and 1884, however, the institution's accession catalog recorded 45,000 specimens of a total of 75,000 items received during this period (Hinsley 72). Indeed, the collecting by the Smithsonian reached such proportions that it threatened the artistic production of individual tribes. For instance, "the Smithsonian's taking of 6,500 pots out of Zuni and Acoma within six years (1880–85) destabilized pottery making traditions, as design sources were removed from the pueblos" (Berlo 3). The Smithsonian's role in supporting and publishing scholarly works on Indian languages and archaeology (Hinsley 47ff.) and its highly visible role in displaying Indian artifacts at the Centennial Exposition in Philadelphia (Rydell 22) are clear evidence that Cather misrepresents the institution's efforts to preserve and publicize Indian cultures.

Cather's own acknowledgment in the novel that Fechtig "was afraid of having trouble getting curiosities out of the United States ports" (215), a fear that inspired his hasty flight across the Mexican border, weakens her charge of bureaucratic indifference to America's aboriginal treasures. Even though no comprehensive laws existed to protect archaeological finds prior to the passing of the Antiquities Act of 1906, public opinion had begun to turn against the unregulated excavation of prehistoric sites, as Nordenskiöld discovered in 1891 when he attempted to remove the Mesa Verde artifacts to the Swedish Consulate in New York (Harrell 120–22). His arrest and the temporary confiscation of the materials he had uncovered with the Wetherills' help are very likely the historical events that explain why Cather has Fechtig escape with his treasures through Mexico.

Since the early 1880s, preservationists had been concerned that important archaeological sites were being destroyed by vandals and unauthorized pothunters, and eventually the General Land Office in the Department of the Interior realized the importance of protecting prehistoric remains (Rothman 15). In 1889, one year after Richard Wetherill's Mesa Verde discovery, Sen. George F. Hoar of Massachusetts petitioned the Senate to pass legislation designed to protect the Casa Grande ruins in Arizona as a culturally significant site. This effort at historic preservation came to fruition in 1892 with the establishment of the Casa Grande Ruins Reservation (Rothman 12). However, more legislation was needed than the protection of individual historic sites. Interesting in the context of Cather's novel is that Richard Wetherill became the catalyst for federal legislation to protect southwestern sites and relics that culminated in the Antiquities Act of 1906.

To be fair to Cather, despite the impression she creates that no one in America cared about Indian artifacts, she does have Tom castigate Roddy on the grounds that the artifacts cannot be considered the private property of the finder. Tom admonishes Roddy: "they weren't mine to sell—nor yours! They belonged to this country, to the state, and to all the people" (219). This statement articulates the growing sentiment that prehistoric remains were a national treasure that only scientists, not profit-oriented amateur archaeologists, should be allowed to access. Hal Rothman sums up this growing conflict as follows:

> But as the collections he [Wetherill] made began to attract the atten-
> tion of anthropologists at universities and museums, Wetherill's name
> became notorious. When the collection the Wetherills made with Nor-
> denskiold appeared in Sweden, American scientists howled. Wetherill
> offended their professional pride and they became nationalistic as they
> publicly castigated him. Simply put, his presence at southwestern sites
> threatened the fledgling profession of anthropology, and his work with
> foreigners gave the anthropologists an avenue to attack him. A dramatic
> powerplay evolved, with Richard Wetherill at its center. He became
> anathema to American anthropologists, epitomizing chaos in the world
> of order they sought to create. (18–19)

While Cather articulates the preservationist sentiment through Tom, she paints Roddy as the villain who sells out America's prehistoric heritage. This contrast has led Philip Gerber to associate Roddy with the attitude of Richard and Al Wetherill, whereas Tom reflects the behavior of John and Clayton Wetherill (116). Yet while Roddy, after his falling out with Tom, disappears from Blue Mesa and the pages of the novel, his real-life counterpart, Richard Wetherill, remained a thorn in the side of preservationists. His involvement with Nordenskiöld at Mesa Verde and his later role in the Hyde expedition galvanized preservation efforts that sought to put commercially motivated explorers like Wetherill out of business. Cather omits any mention of this fascinating part of Richard Wetherill's life, perhaps because it would have made it harder for her to chide America as a culturally second-rate country unconcerned with its prehistoric heritage. (The campaign to put an end to Richard Wetherill's exploration and appropriation of Indian artifacts, culminating in the passage of the Antiquities Act of 1906, is described in Lee, *Antiquities Act of 1906*. For a highly negative portrayal of Richard Wetherill's activities, see Rothman.)

It appears that Cather, to convey more dramatically to her readers that the preservation of Indian art as a national treasure was of utmost importance, deliberately omits any mention of legislative efforts to protect antiquities in *The Professor's House* and misrepresents the Smithsonian Institution. To gauge just how significant the connection between Native American cultures and American art is for Cather, one need only look at the Panther Canyon scene in *The Song of the Lark*. Here, Thea Kronborg finds her voice and identity as an American artist in the spiritual presence of ancient Anasazi women who created beautiful pieces of pottery out of local clay. Cather contends that American art must take into account the works of the first American artists who turned the earth into purposeful vessels and then into objects of art. Pointing to the human urge to create art, Cather writes: "Food, fire, water and something else—even here, in this crack in the world, so far back in the night of the past! Down here at the beginning, that painful thing was already stirring; the seed of sorrow, and of so much delight" (279–80). Thea has stumbled upon one of the cradles of American art. The potsherds she collects "were like fetters that bound one to a long chain of human endeavour," to "help to fulfil some desire of the dust that slept there" (280). If one applies this notion to *The Professor's House*, the loss of the artifacts, their material and artistic value aside, manifests the removal of a root that, in Cather's mind, is vital to American art and culture.

Cather's comments in her 1924 *New York Times* interview with Rose C. Feld may further explain why she downplayed American interest in aboriginal art and emphasized foreign interest in it. It seems that when she wrote *The Professor's House* she was deeply disillusioned with American culture, and her fatigue with it is mirrored in that of her protagonist, Godfrey St. Peter. To express her disdain, she compares America unflatteringly to Europe. For instance, Cather contrasts French sophistication with America's intellectual and artistic mediocrity, a strategy that serves the same purpose as her claim that Germany shows more interest than America in the appropriation of Indian artifacts, namely, to vent her frustration with a perceived decline of American culture.

Specifically, Cather praises the French Academy for maintaining "a great purity of tradition" by judging the accomplishments of young artists against the genius of established ones. She told the *New York Times*: "It is good sense, deliberation and an eagerness for the beautiful that keeps up the fine front of French art. That is true of her literature as well as of her painting" (Feld 11). It is hard to escape the irony that Cather praises France's cultural sophistication in this 1924 interview while at the same time denouncing Dr. Ripley, the secretary of the Smithsonian in *The Professor's House*, for planning a trip to "an International Exposition of some sort in Europe" (212) which Harrell identifies as either the International Paris Exposition of 1900 or the Paris Exposition of 1889 (117–18). Yet there is no doubt that Cather expected American art to draw on its own tradition. This is evident from her praise for Whistler and Whitman, who, in an effort to revive art, had "caught the flame of former years and are carrying the torch into the next period" (Feld 11). Cather makes no reference to Native American art in the interview, but in the light of Thea Kronborg's transformation into an American artist among the silent remains of the Anasazi, it is apparent that Cather saw aboriginal art as an important source for an American artistic tradition. To ignore it, or worse, to sell it, was a symptom of America's cultural malaise that she needed to expose.

There is a final irony of which Cather was probably not aware. In 1911, German expressionist Emil Nolde drew and painted Hopi kachina dolls and other tribal objects in the Museum of Ethnology in Berlin (Lloyd 173, 178) and later incorporated them into a series of still lifes. Nolde was among a number of European avant-garde painters who appropriated tribal art to transform and revitalize modern artistic expression. Had she known about this, Cather would have considered it powerful support for her case that Native American art could provide a source of inspiration for American art at large.

This attempt to track down the destination of Fechtig's curios illustrates that Cather did her homework in establishing the connection between Germany and Mesa Verde and the Wetherills. It is also evident that she took great liberties with the facts when doing so suited her purpose. Clearly, the profound pessimism with which she looked upon American culture in the mid-1920s legitimized her creation of the impression that Native American art was held in low esteem in America. What better strategy to rail against such imagined indifference than to point at a foreign agent who is emptying the national treasure chest and carrying off a vital source of artistic inspiration to Germany?

Marilee Lindemann

Fear of a Queer Mesa?

Faith, Friendship, and National Sexuality in "Tom Outland's Story"

"How'm I gonna know 'bout you? They might kill ya an' I wouldn' know. They might hurt ya. How'm I gonna know?"...

"[I]t don' matter.... [I]'ll be all aroun' in the dark. I'll be ever'where—wherever you look. Wherever they's a fight so hungry people can eat, I'll be there. Wherever they's a cop beatin' up a guy, I'll be there.... I'll be in the way kids laugh when they're hungry an' they know supper's ready. An' when our folks eat the stuff they raise an' live in the houses they build—why, I'll be there. See?"–John Steinbeck, The Grapes of Wrath

This essay enters into several critical conversations at once in an effort to get at underexamined aspects of *The Professor's House*. My analysis is firstly and happily a kind of riff on aspects of sex and citizenship explored by Lauren Berlant in her brilliant *The Queen of America Goes to Washington City*. Specifically, I'm interested in her notion of the "pilgrimage to Washington" as a favorite American plot, a test of what she calls "citizenship competence" (24) in which a childlike citizen visiting the capital confronts "the tension between utopia and history" and, because of his or her innocence and naïveté, "unsettles[s], expose[s], and reframe[s] the machinery of national life" (28–29). Secondly, my analysis builds on recent lesbian/gay/queer engagements with Cather by, for example, Eve Kosofsky Sedgwick, Judith Butler, Christopher Nealon, and Jonathan Goldberg that have usefully complicated the image of Cather as a homophobic lesbian who either wrote from the closet or wrote nothing at all on the matter of sexuality. (Sedgwick briefly addresses *The Professor's House* in her essay on the crisscrossings of gender and sexuality and the refractions of desire in Cather [174–76], as does Butler in her discussion of Cather's masculine names and "the destabilization of gender and sexuality through the name" [144]. Nealon offers a trenchant critique of Walter Benn Michaels in the course of his discussion of the novel [27–31]. Goldberg's more extended analysis of *The Professor's House* dovetails in many respects with my own, particularly in its emphasis on Tom's contradictory position as "both inside and out; the homosexual lining of the heterosexual as well as the homosexual irritant to the heterosexual" [472].)

Thirdly, my analysis is a reply to Walter Benn Michaels's provocative yet reductive reading in *Our America* of Cather's all-male families (like the one established by Tom, Roddy, and Henry Atkins on the mesa) as a trope of the nativist desire for racial purity, for it eliminates the threat of miscegenation by eliminating the possibility of reproduction. Homosexuality thus serves, according to Michaels, as "the model for a purified Americanism," a crucial technology "in the effort to prevent half-breeds" (48–49). Finally, these remarks may supply not a counter but a complement to my own reading of *The Professor's House* in *Willa Cather: Queering America*, my study of Cather's entanglements in early-twentieth-century discourses of sexuality and nation. There I discussed the story of Godfrey St. Peter as an allegory of male authority and misogyny in a masculinist culture, an allegory tied to Cather's anxieties in the 1920s about the increasingly marginalized place of women writers in post–World War I formations of American literary history (100–114). Here I would like to focus more closely on the same-sex relationship that is in many respects the affective core of the novel, the friendship between Tom Outland and Roddy Blake.

Sedgwick has described this relationship as a "gorgeous homosocial romance" (174), which it is, but its gorgeousness is also marked by profound uncertainty and by repeated allusions to the nation that surrounds the mesa. Tom's betrayal of his friendship with Roddy is set into motion, for example, by his pilgrimage to the nation's capital, where he finds selfish bureaucrats instead of the insightful archaeologist whom Father Duchene had predicted would help Tom and Roddy "throw light on some important points in the history of your country" (199). In their showdown over Roddy's sale of the artifacts, Roddy (rightly) accuses Tom of assaulting him with "Fourth of July talk" (221) that masks both Tom's assertion of power over Roddy and his claim to the artifacts as his private property. These intrusions of the national into the "world above the world" (217) that is the mesa effectively destroy the paradise of male intimacy that had been established there, leaving Tom happy but alone with his Virgil in the short run and "not very sanguine" (229) about his prospects for good fortune in the long run. In this essay, I would like to explore how anxieties about sexuality and nationality combine to thwart the utopian homoeroticism of the Blue Mesa.

What I will be doing, then, is looking at *The Professor's House* through the lens I used in the first part of *Queering America*—that is, considering Cather's entanglement in processes of national self-imaging and her fascination with the semiotics of American bodies and physical spaces—such as prairies and mesas—that serve as synecdoches of the nation. Do we see here similar tensions over sameness and difference, between a corporeal utopianism inherited from Whitman and a corporeal dystopianism that seems tied to the Progressive Era's mania for social hygiene as well as to, perhaps, the nativism of the postwar period? How would I answer Michaels's reading by looking at this text rather than away from it, as I did in *Queering America*, at other texts? Do we see any evidence here of a technology for the creation of racial and sexual *ambiguity*, which is how I argued the discourse of "Bohemianism" functioned in *My Ántonia*? Given the fairly obvious homoerotic investments of the novel, who can be said to occupy the space of the "queer," and what does that occupation mean? How do queer bodies signify, and what vision of nation is ratified or repressed in their so signifying?

It cannot be argued that *The Professor's House* is fully at ease with the world of differences it calls into being. In this respect, it is markedly unlike *The Song of the Lark* and *Death Comes for the Archbishop*, novels in which differences—of culture, character, or body—are for the most part positively valued as agents or signifiers of challenge and change. One thinks, for example, of the marvelous and much-remarked-upon corporeality of Thea Kronborg, the larger-than-life diva who shakes up the sex-race-gender system of her culture and provokes in her thrilled audience a response "almost savage in its fierceness" (569). Similarly, the "homely, . . . poorly built," yet energetic body of Joseph Vaillant is an extremely effective agent for realizing the utopian fantasy of cross-cultural syncretism that impels *Death Comes for the Archbishop*. By contrast, *The Professor's House* is a grouchy book whose narrative—and not just the characters within it—is punctuated by moments of nativism, anti-Semitism, misogyny, and homophobia. It is bitchy about everything from the war and Prohibition to education and consumerism. I will not speculate in this essay on the authorial roots of this pervasive bitterness (though Hermione Lee [224–58] offers a subtle and compelling biographical reading of *The Professor's House*) but will focus instead on its social and cultural implications and on the tug-of-war that goes on in the text between anxiety and optimism over the changing character of the American body politic.

The Blue Mesa is the space in the novel in which bodies, families, and nations are radically reimagined. It is a "queer" space, I would argue, in that it is an "out-land," a space in which, instead of two men and a baby, as a popular film once put it, we have three guys and a mummy setting up a household, doing the mostly fun work of being cowboys and archaeologists, and building "a happy family," as Tom puts it (176), a family bearing little resemblance to the kinship-based web of jealousies, disappointments, and "cruel biological necessities" (13) that characterizes St. Peter's family. "Pal[s]" (164), "stray[s]" (165), and "castaway[s]" (175), the three men establish a haven of domesticity and adventure, simplicity and "luxury" (169), where life is a "holiday," home is a "playhouse," and "good behavior" is a simple matter of avoiding liquor and knowing how to make plain bunks "feel like a Harvey House bed" (176). Michaels, as I have already noted, reads the mesa family as an emblem of the nativist desire for pure bloodlines, which to some extent it probably is. It is also, however, an emblem or a technology of sex and gender ambiguity, a homological space where *sameness* signifies not just racial purity but also the potential for a sexual blending of like with like that calls into question the naturalness and the compulsory character of heterosexuality. On the axis of race, Louie Marsellus is the greatest threat to the purity of St. Peter's and the "American" family, since "the Jew" is so emphatically marked in the text as "foreign" to "the family circle" (64). The mesa family is from that standpoint an ideal alternative to the threat of racial intermixture. However, on the axis of sex and gender, Tom, out on the queer Blue Mesa with Roddy and Henry, is equal parts threat and dream, representing as he does freedom from the profoundly corrosive social machinery that the weary Professor finds the regime of heterosexuality to be. This is why Tom must ultimately be brought off the mesa and inculcated with a different set of "family values," which culminates in his engagement to Rosamond St. Peter and his death in a war waged to defend those values.

Tom's "pilgrimage to Washington" is the first step in the young man's deadly reeducation and in the destruction of the mesa as an achieved utopia, so it is worth considering in some detail, though readers of *The Professor's House*, myself included, typically overlook it. Tom's journey is undertaken at the behest of Roddy, who expects the national government to reward the two cowpunchers for their discoveries on the mesa, and of Father Duchene, who expects the government to send out "the proper specialists" to study the remains and "revive this civilization in a scholarly work" (199). Tom is a perfect example of Berlant's "infantile citizen," for he comes to the capital city armed with innocence and expectation and is imbued with "a very religious feeling" the moment he steps off the train and sees the white dome of the Capitol against the blue sky of a "cold bright January morning" (203). (If the reader will pardon a personal aside, I cannot help mentioning that Tom's reaction here reminds me of my seven-year-old nephew who came to visit me in the summer of 1999 to undertake his own first pilgrimage to Washington. On being driven through the city on our way home from the airport, Collin caught his first glimpse of the Washington Monument and said, after a sharp intake of breath, "Doesn't it make you feel great to be an American when you see this stuff?") Tom's initial experience of the nation is, like Collin's, a sentimental one. It is important to note that his "religious feeling[s]" are transferred from the Capitol to the mesa after his disappointment in Washington and his break with Roddy, as he experiences "a religious emotion" (226) in being on the mesa alone with his *Aeneid* after Roddy leaves. Like so many of Cather's male characters, Tom is unable to bear disillusionment, unable to transform his unreflective national sentimentality into a more realistic, critical, ambivalent form of national knowledge. He realizes what Berlant describes as "the potential catastrophe of all visits to Washington." "Can national identification," Berlant asks, "survive the practical habitation of everyday life in the national locale? Can the citizen/tourist gain the critical skills for living nationality without losing faith in the nation-state's capacity to provide the wisdom and justice it promises" (29)? In Tom's case, the answer to these questions would seem to be no, for he slinks out of town depressed and ashamed, having failed in his mission and having spent all the money Roddy had staked him (213). He is subsequently uncomfortable even speaking about his time in Washington and stubbornly refuses to consider a scholarship to Johns Hopkins for graduate study, insisting that Baltimore is "all wrong for me" and "always made me blue" (153). Apparently, mere proximity to the capital is sufficient to activate Tom's lingering national malaise.

Let's look more closely at Tom's pilgrimage, its effects, and its contexts in order to complicate the story I have been telling and to keep from setting up an overly neat opposition between the "good" mesa and the "bad" capital city. That Tom is able so smoothly to transfer his "religious feeling" about the Capitol to the mesa suggests that the two spaces are linked not through opposition or contrast but through another instance of homologic—that is, Cather here is linking like with like. Instances of physical resemblance between the mesa and the capital city are numerous and substantial. Federal Washington is, like the cliff dwellings on the Blue Mesa, a "city of stone" that can seem to be "asleep" (179) on quiet Sunday mornings and during periods of political lassitude. The mesa is, like Washington, in some ways monumental. John Rapp, the foreman for the cattle company Tom and Roddy work for, warns them that the mesa is inaccessible because its cliffs "are like the base of a monument, all the way round" (169). Tom first sees the cliff dwellings, as he first sees the Capitol, in the light of a cold winter morning. Both spaces are relatively small and contained, carefully designed, and built out of white stone. Both are produced by civilizations that value, as Father Duchene puts it, "order and security" (199). That Tom shares these values is evident in the sights he sees in Washington and emphasizes in his narrative: the Capitol, where laws are made; the treasury, which oversees the nation's economic security; the army and the navy, which assure its military security; the White House, home to the head of state; and the Washington Monument, which honors the first head of state and the mythical "father" of the nation. (Of course, Tom's choices as a tourist are somewhat more limited than they would be today. In the first decade of the twentieth century, he would not have been able to visit the monuments to the more radically democratic presidents, Thomas Jefferson and Abraham Lincoln, because they were not yet built. The monuments to the nation's founding philosopher of egalitarianism and its great emancipator were completed in 1943 and 1922, respectively.)

Interestingly, what Tom notices about the White House is the fence that "shuts in" the grounds, as well, perhaps, as the man who lives there, while he recalls the "shaft" of the monument "pink" in the light of the city's sunsets. That pink shaft dominates the scene and Tom's memory of the city, an image of the male potency lacking in the clerks who stream out of the government buildings and seem to Tom "like people in slavery" (211), and in Tom himself, who spends days in Washington waiting for appointments with nothing to do but "stud[y] the patterns of the rugs" (205) in various waiting rooms. What proves so catastrophic for Tom is the unbearable contrast between what Berlant terms "the sublimity of national identity" (25), which he experiences during his "wonderfully happy" (203) week as a tourist in the city, and the ordinariness of living, working, and trying to get things done in the complex machinery of the federal bureaucracy. During this frustrating period, when he is hanging out with "girls who wanted to get typewriting to do, [and] nice polite old men who wanted to be taken out on surveys and expeditions next summer" (205), Tom comes to see citizenship as a form of abjection.

The citizen-as-supplicant is feminized/emasculated in his dependence upon the state as dispenser of jobs, money, and favors. Even the director of the Smithsonian proves to be abject in his desire to secure government financing for a trip to an international exposition in Europe. Tom's discomfort in this role is similar to the dis-ease "Hawthorne" articulates in the "Custom-House" essay about his brief career as a government employee. Describing "Uncle Sam's gold" as "the Devil's wages," Hawthorne claimed that working for the state robbed the soul of "its sturdy force, its courage and constancy, its truth, its self-reliance, and all that gives the emphasis to manly character" (33). The depression that marks Tom's exit from Washington suggests that in his view his soul is similarly sapped not by working for but by waiting for Uncle Sam.

Tom's disappointment in Washington acquires even greater resonance when we consider that, by the loose chronology established in the novel, his trip would have occurred around 1905 or 1906, in the middle of Teddy Roosevelt's bustling tenure as president. (In his detailed chronology of *The Professor's House* [217], David Harrell, who is more careful and consistent than either Cather or Tom, establishes Tom's trip to Washington as taking place from January through June of 1906.) This coincidence invests the young man's feelings of impotence and emasculation with irony and a national significance that helps to clarify the politics of sexuality that animate *The Professor's House*. In the first decade of the twentieth century, "Washington City," as Lillian St. Peter calls it (152), was imbued with Roosevelt's optimism and enthusiasm and embarked upon an ambitious plan for beautifying the city and reviving Pierre L'Enfant's original designs for it, according to Constance McLaughlin Green's lively and thorough account in *Washington: Capital City, 1879–1950* (132–70). Many of the buildings completed during this period were neoclassical in design and built of marble or pale gray granite, which gave the city a uniform and monumental look—a look that seems to have impressed Tom and that prompted Cather to describe Washington as "this clean, white city" (Curtin 829–30) in a piece she wrote during a stay of several months in 1900 and 1901, just months before McKinley's assassination made Roosevelt president. (For an account of Cather's time in Washington, see Woodress 147–49. For reprints of the columns Cather produced for the *Nebraska State Journal* and the *Index of Pittsburgh Life*, see Curtin 792–835.) Cleanliness was not just part of the look of Washington; it was on the city's moral and social agenda as well. Programs of social betterment were combined with efforts to improve housing and increase economic opportunities for the city's poor in the hope of eradicating the slums hidden in alleys "within a stone's throw of the Capitol" (Green 148). Cather was either oblivious to the effects of such poverty or optimistic about the various campaigns to improve urban conditions. She remarks in a column on Christmas in the capital that "Even the beggars in this easy-going, good-natured city are never the unfortunate degenerated creatures that they are elsewhere" (Curtin 802). Tom makes no mention of beggars, focusing instead on the spiritual impoverishment of the "hundreds of little black-coated men pouring out of white buildings" (213) at the end of the government's workday.

Teddy Roosevelt obviously presided over a good deal more than the transformation of Washington into a model for America's "city beautiful" movement (Green 133). As I have already noted, during Tom's periods of "low-spiritedness" in Washington, he walks "for hours around the fence that shuts in the White House grounds" (211), perhaps hoping to restore his vitality by getting close to the famously energetic former Rough Rider. In a study of how race and gender were deployed in turn-of-the-century discourses of American civilization, Gail Bederman has deftly analyzed Roosevelt's pivotal role as advocate and incarnation of a model of virile manhood intended to counter anxieties about effeminacy and overcivilization and to advance U.S. interests in the causes of nationalism and imperialism. Significantly, as early as the 1890s and throughout his presidency, Roosevelt's pronouncements on the virtues of the morally and physically "strenuous life" invoked the specter of "race suicide" in order to impress upon (white) audiences their (hetero)sexual duty to the state and to civilization. Bederman reports that by 1903 Roosevelt's campaigning on the issue of "race suicide"—fears that America's white racial stock was being diluted through declining birthrates and the changing demographics of immigration—earned him a reputation with the public as "a patron saint of large families" (203). Indeed, in a 1911 column on the subject of "race decadence," the former president described any marriage that produced fewer than four children as "sterile," claiming that "The race cannot go ahead, it will not keep its numbers even, unless the average man and woman who are married and who are capable of having children have a family of four children. These, and these only, are the men and women with whom the whole future of the nation, the whole future of civilization, rests" (DiNunzio 341). Instead of the Victorian ethic of sexual restraint, Roosevelt, despite his own prudishness, helped to affirm the potency of American civilization by affirming, as Bederman puts it, "the sexual power of American manhood" (203). Roosevelt, with his six children in the White House and his unique combination of "manliness (morality) and masculinity (sexuality)," came as close as anyone could to "publicly praising male sexuality as an intrinsic aspect of powerful masculinity" (Bederman 205).

For Tom, the only child of parents too weak to survive the journey west (his father drowned and his mother succumbed to illness [105]), Roosevelt's insistence that marital procreation was a citizen's duty to the nation would no doubt have been a vexing executive order. Tom's dispirited walks around the White House bring Roosevelt into the story, even though he is never identified as president in Tom's narrative. He may be a spectral presence, but he is nonetheless an important one, for he functions as a fatherly authority figure from the world of politics and government much as Father Duchene and Godfrey St. Peter served for Tom as fatherly authorities from the worlds of religion and academia, respectively. Viewed in this light, Tom's restless walking through the streets of Washington marks him as the modern neurasthenic against whom Roosevelt and others railed. His longing to leave Washington and "get back to the mesa and live a free life and breathe free air" (213) is a longing to return to his version of Roosevelt's fantastic construction of the American West as a space of manly, salubrious activity. The language in which Tom expresses his longing to return to the mesa even echoes the kind of language Roosevelt used to describe the lives of ranchmen and cowboys in his extensive writings about the West in the 1880s. In *Hunting Trips of a Ranchman* (1885), for example, TR praised "the free, open-air life of the ranchman" as "the pleasantest and healthiest life in America" (qtd. in DiNunzio 282).

Tom's return is complicated, though, as returns often are, by the fact that he has been changed by his pilgrimage to Washington and that the mesa itself has changed in his absence. He claims that he leaves Washington "wiser than I came" (213). The wisdom he takes back to the mesa with him is not simply that politics is often a petty game of competing, selfish interests. It is also that "manliness (morality)" without "masculinity ([hetero]sexuality)" is socially useless and possibly depraved, that the "free life" of the cowboy acquires significance only when the strength and skills it develops are dedicated to forging and expanding the (white, heterosexual) American nation. Homophobia figured implicitly or explicitly into much of the discourse of manliness and civilization as Roosevelt and others deployed it. Bederman notes that Roosevelt's very self-conscious efforts to "masculiniz[e] his image" in the early 1880s by representing himself as the "Cowboy of the Dakotas" were motivated by newspaper attacks in which the young New York State assemblyman was lampooned as effeminate and often referred to as Oscar Wilde (170–71). One could argue, then, that Roosevelt's whole public persona as well as his arduous campaigning for manliness and prolific heterosexuality were motivated by a clear instance of homosexual panic. Thus, I would suggest, Tom is "utterly ashamed to go home to Roddy" (213) in part because he has acquired a new and homophobic understanding of their "happy family," which helps to account for both the virulence of his attack on Roddy and for the efforts he makes throughout the story he tells St. Peter to portray himself as squeaky clean and even "straight," in no way bent or queer. "What [Roddy] needed," Tom explains in justifying their friendship, "was . . . a straight fellow to give an account to" (164). Indeed.

My point in emphasizing the similarities between Tom's constructions of and responses to Washington and the Blue Mesa and his receptiveness to Roosevelt's sex/gender message is to suggest that Tom is from the beginning (because the "beginning" of his narrative is after his trip to Washington) less free than St. Peter imagines him to be, less queer, as it were, than I might wish him to be. With his love of law, order, and male potency, Tom simply yet forcefully transfers his sentimental patriotism, leavened by a heavy dose of Rooseveltian heteronormativity, from Washington to the mesa, which destroys his relationship with Roddy as well as the radically democratic, Whitmanesque dream of comradely love that their relationship briefly concretized. Roddy will have none of Tom's "Fourth of July talk," seeming to recognize it as a cheap souvenir of Tom's trip to Washington and as the betrayal it is. After this key point in the chronology of his life—which is different from the order of Cather's narrative—Tom moves with a strange combination of mindlessness and eagerness toward precisely the kind of death-in-life that so appalled him when he saw it among the government clerks in Washington. The novel is nearly silent on why the character previously defined by his mobility and by his fondness for wide open spaces is suddenly willing to be, like the man in the White House, fenced in—walled in by the Professor's French garden, his table manners monitored by the punctilious Lillian St. Peter, his face flushed by the rapt attention of two little girls. "There was evidently something enchanting about the atmosphere of the house to a boy who had always lived a rough life" (106) is all the narrative offers by way of explanation. St. Peter, of course, finds the atmosphere of his house noxious, yet he picks up Tom's bag to "prevent his escape" from it the first time he comes to see the Professor (99). The details of Tom's later courtship of and engagement to Rosamond St. Peter, as well as of some intrigue involving the other sister, Kathleen, are famously absent, the sexual "things not named" in a novel that is happy to clutter itself with other kinds of detail. We learn a little more about Tom's brilliant success at the university, but nothing very clear on the crucial question of his relationship with Dr. Crane and how Tom could have failed to make some provision in his will to assure that his teacher would share in the profits from the gas he invented in Crane's laboratory, though he had the forethought to secure a patent on the invention. "I don't think it occurred to the boy that the will would ever be probated," is all St. Peter has to say on the subject (118). Finally, Tom rushes off to the war, again seeming a bit mindless and overly eager, because Father Duchene stops to see him on his way back to Belgium determined to serve in any capacity he might. The impressionable Tom sails off with him and dies a year later in Flanders.

"There was an ache in my arms to reach out and detain him," remarks Tom as Roddy climbs down to the river and out of his life on the night of their argument, "but there was something else that made me absolutely powerless to do so" (223). As is so often the case in Cather, the "something else" that makes such a difference in Tom's life is pointedly unspecified. I would suggest that what thwarts Tom here is the same failure of will and imagination that prevents him from transforming his disillusionment in Washington into an active and resistant notion of citizenship, from turning his sentimental nationality into a thoroughly queer and participatory nationality. Instead, Tom, perhaps unwittingly, becomes the agent of the violent suppression of the homoerotic boyhood that he, Roddy, and that "mannerly old boy" Henry (176) share on the mesa, a suppression undertaken in the interest of reproducing the kind of heterosexual national manhood embodied in such dutiful, depressed husbands and fathers as Godfrey St. Peter and in such committed eugenicists as Teddy Roosevelt. St. Peter, too, is paralyzed by his inability to enact a vital notion of citizenship, a citizenship that might be capable of messing up and perhaps reframing the machineries of the national life he finds so oppressive. The results of his emotional crisis are wholly negative and articulated strictly in the private terms of family, though his emphasis on "the secondary *social* man, the lover" (240) as the catalyst of the "chain of events" leading to his sense of entrapment in an unreal life at least acknowledges "the family" as a public, political entity. The best he can achieve, however, is a renunciation, a letting go of "something very precious" (258). The only survival strategy he can imagine is to figure out a way to live "without delight," a strategy whose national implications are made clear in St. Peter's sardonically linking it to having "to learn to live without sherry" "in a Prohibition country" (257).

St. Peter's unspecified "something very precious" recalls the "something else" that prevented Tom from relieving the ache in his arms by reaching out for his beloved friend in their moment of crisis. In the present tense of the novel, Roddy is the true enigma, the absent presence known only through Tom's stories, and the object of many desires and quests. (The absence of Tom is different. His death is mourned, but his fate is known. Roddy's is not.) Louie still searches for him. Kitty still dreams of finding him, and St. Peter believes he ought to search for him because "He's on my conscience" (112). If in the end, part of what St. Peter renounces is Roddy's claim on his conscience, Roddy still haunts the political unconscious of Cather's novel. He is out there, somewhere, and part of his allure is that he, unlike Tom, remained true to the mesa's queer code of loyalty to chosen relationships over blood kinship. Tom has come to view the latter as superior, sniffing that Roddy "ought to have had boys of his own to look after. Nature's full of such substitutions, but they always seem to me sad, even in botany" (165). That cruel and gratuitous remark, whether or not it is a measure of Cather's or the text's homophobia, is certainly a measure of Tom's homophobia, of his desire to distance himself from the intimacy and intensity of his bond with Roddy in telling St. Peter his story. It is also the clearest indication of how completely Tom has internalized the Rooseveltian model of national sexuality as heterosexual and prolifically reproductive, since Tom insists that Roddy ought to have had not one but several "boys of his own." Looming out there somewhere just off the edge of the text's political horizons, Roddy may be imagined as a kind of Tom Joad figure (as Tom describes himself to Ma Joad in the passage I have used as an epigraph), still on the move and looking after vulnerable boys in a series of substitutions that are anything but sad. With his stubborn loyalty, his obsessive newspaper reading, and his thoughtful brooding "on the great injustices of his time" (166), Roddy stands in the text for the possibility of vital, activist, even insurgent citizenship. Through Tom, Roddy makes a vicarious pilgrimage to Washington and is similarly disappointed that there seemed to be no one there that "cared a damn" (219) about their discoveries. Unlike Tom, however, Roddy turns his disappointment into action, though the action of selling off the artifacts is admittedly troubling. Of greater importance, though, is that Roddy leaves the mesa when Tom has destroyed for him the reality of their "happy family," refusing to be treated like "a hired man" (222) by someone he had considered an equal. He storms out and takes with him all the mesa's queer utopian possibilities and is never heard from again. Tom stays and takes possession of the mesa as the locus of an emphatically un-queer and merely sentimental nationality. His arms will ache, I would wager, with unfulfilled longings and unimagined political possibilities for a very long time to come.

John J. Murphy

Holy Cities, Poor Savages, and the Science Culture

Positioning *The Professor's House*

Sojourns in France framed a personal occasion for Cather that must be considered in an evaluation of *The Professor's House* and its Mesa Verde story. Her five-month stay in 1920 focused on medieval Paris and Provence, though presumably she was gathering material for a contemporary novel. In 1923 she returned to France, again for several months, and, according to Lewis, conceived *The Professor's House* at Aix-les-Bains: "She did not work there, but it was perhaps in the peace and beauty of the Savoie countryside that the idea of [the novel] took shape" (133). Between these visits—on 27 December 1922, one of the last days in the year when she claimed the world broke in two and she "slid back into yesterday's seven thousand years" (*Not Under Forty*, prefatory note)—she was confirmed with her parents in Red Cloud's Episcopal church. In *The Professor's House* Cather relieves her midwestern locale by including French and southwestern settings, subdues the romantic aestheticism that inspires *The Song of the Lark*, and uses the mesa and its canyons as a setting for anguish as much as revelation. The problems of the protagonists in *The Professor's House* reflect crises Cather herself had experienced and resolved between her two Anasazi-inspired novels, crises at once broadly cultural as well as personally spiritual.

Prologue

Cather's fascination with southwestern mesas, as is suggested in Jean Latour's recognition of their resemblance to Gothic cathedrals in *Death Comes for the Archbishop*, can be traced to the architecture and topography she appreciated during her visit to Europe in 1902, ten years before she was introduced to the American Southwest. The highlight of her sojourn in England seems to have been the Chester cathedral, where in the cloister she imagined "the order of prayers and offices and penances . . . never broken" through history's cataclysms (Curtin 896). In Paris, this enthusiasm was increased by the "white gleam of Sacre-Coeur" on Montmartre, which reminded Cather of "the city of St. John's vision or the Heavenly City that Bunyan saw across the river" (924). Anticipating Archbishop Latour's introduction to Ácoma (and her own discovery of Quebec City), she would discover on Avignon's Doms Rock, beetling above the Rhone, a twelfth-century Romanesque cathedral, the Palace of the Popes (who resided there from 1309 to 1377), and a garden offering sunset views of the distant Alps to the east. Avignon's rock had been the locale of human settlement since the Neolithic era, one that had developed into a flourishing port by the fifth century B.C. Its fourteenth-century palace, as Edith Lewis reports, "stirred [Cather] as no building in the world had ever done" (190).

   In 1912 Cather first visited the mesa country. Using as her base Winslow, Arizona, where her brother Douglass shared a bungalow with another Santa Fe Railroad worker, she explored cliff dwellings in Walnut Canyon, visited Mexican communities and remote missions, and heard Spanish and Indian legends from Winslow's priest. Cather now had "a new Spanish world to think of—and eventually write of" (83), recalls Elizabeth Sergeant of this first southwestern encounter. The "grandiose and historical scale" of this world forecast "some great spiritual event" to Cather, "something . . . that had nothing to do with the appalling mediocrity and vulgarity of [contemporary American] industrial civilization" (81–82). Not surprisingly, Cather compared the Southwest to France, the country that offered her similar reprieve from claustrophobic aspects of American (especially Nebraskan) life. She wrote Sergeant that the Albuquerque area resembled "the country between Marseilles and Nice but [was] more luminous. Even finer than the Rhone Valley. . . . She described Indian villages set around Spanish Mission churches" (81). Visiting the cliff dwellings, Cather was "deeply . . . stirred" by contact with an "age-old but . . . intensely near and akin civilization" (Lewis 81).

   This first visit to the Southwest resulted, according to Sergeant, in Cather's sudden "control of inner creative forces." Somehow, "the vast solitude of the Southwest, its bald magnificence, brilliant light and physical impact, too, had the effect of toning up [Cather's] spirit, and made available a path in which a new artistic method could evolve from familiar Nebraska subject matter" (85). The result was *O Pioneers!* and Cather's discovery of herself as an artist. To Thea Kronborg in *The Song of the Lark* Cather bequeathed the aesthetic epiphany she experienced in the southwestern canyons, and she later tapped it for Tom Outland's first night alone on the mesa. But memories of France (especially of Avignon) remained with Cather to satisfy other than aesthetic yearnings, for the canyons also had challenged her to "measur[e herself] with that ancient image, Death, which so easily overpowered a white man in this environment" (Sergeant 123). Writing to Sergeant in France in 1913 after returning from the Southwest, Cather "mourn[ed] that she was not . . . drinking a *petit verre* in the Place de la Republique" and recalled "the little willows of Avignon resting their elbows in the flooded Rhone. Her most splendid memory was of the Rocher des Doms and its Virgin [on the cathedral], golden above the great river" (96). These memories were of a comfortable and contained world that offered sanctuary from the consuming (if inspiring), alien world of the Southwest, which had become her setting in part because Europe was inaccessible during World War I. According to Sergeant, when Cather revisited New Mexico in 1914, during the writing of *The Song of the Lark*, she was "in [a] restless, hopeful mood," but "the war cut into her joyous travels, even in the Sangre de Cristo Mountains" (127); with France and all European values threatened, she returned to Pittsburgh.

The concerns of the southwestern section of *The Song of the Lark* are revealing as a prologue to those of the Mesa Verde section of *The Professor's House*. The former are essentially aesthetic and are easily translated into a singer's development. Exhausted from her work routine in Chicago, Thea seeks out a room of her own in the dead, windswept city—from which she has access (via an ancient water trail) to a stream and a bathing pool and from which she can contemplate a half-ruined watchtower used to entice eagles. For her the ancient inhabitants of the ruins symbolize her own misgivings as an artist; these people were timid, their lives sad, monotonous, like the swallows that never rose above the canyon rim. However, the eagle that dips into the canyon and then rises beyond its rim, "steeped in light . . . like a golden bird" (287–88), she relates to her own future success, which will enable the poor Indians whose pottery lies shattered along the stream to soar beyond the rim with her: "O eagle of eagles! Endeavor, achievement, desire, glorious striving of human art!" If glorious, the achievement is, indeed, quite human and quite secular; it also privileges European art (in this case musical) beyond anything achieved by the cliff dwellers, equating that art with religion, as Sherrill Harbison has recently shown. Cather "had adopted the Romantic view of the artist as mediator between human and divine realms as early as her teens" and was now giving it a Wagnerian slant and "elevating [art] to a religion" (xvii–viii).

A few years later, during the postwar malaise, when a now successful Cather returned to France, the arrogance of this view of art had been tempered by more traditional responses to religion and culture. *My Ántonia* (in its own way an expression of war-related malaise) had intervened, as had Cather's weeklong 1915 visit to Mesa Verde, when she spent a day at Cliff Palace ruin (Tom's city) and a night stranded in Soda Canyon. Lewis refers to the hours she spent waiting in the moonlight as "the most rewarding of our whole trip to the Mesa Verde" (97) and affirms them as "the real genesis" of "Tom Outland's Story" (99). Cather's uncertainty, as she reacquainted herself with France for the French section of *One of Ours*, might be revealed through the protagonist of that novel, Claude Wheeler. Claude first considers the American West his opportunity to rise, like Thea's eagle, beyond the restraining walls of materialistic Nebraska life, but he rejects it: "The statue of Kit Carson on horseback, down in the [Denver] Square, pointed Westward; but there was no West, in that sense [of freedom], any more.... Here the sky was like a lid shut down over the world" (100). But much later, when Claude finds himself among a few worshiping women in Rouen's church of St. Ouen and looks up at the rose window and listens to the great bell, "[t]he revelations of the glass and the bell . . . were superlatives toward which his mind had always been groping" (276–77). The liberating experience is set not in the West, in Panther Canyon, but in a European abbey church, and it represents movement from Nebraska to France as well as Cather's development from provincial to world writer.

The Novel's Problem Clusters

There are two complementary problem clusters in *The Professor's House*: one is an imbalance between Godfrey St. Peter's roles as husband/father and professor/scholar (a failure in equilibrium between his "marriages" to his wife and his work), and the other, which is historical and cultural as well as social, involves what Henry Adams began examining at the Paris Exposition of 1900 as the opposed forces of the dynamo and the Virgin.

In her letter on the novel's form, Cather cited the combination in certain Dutch paintings of interior and window scenes, a juxtaposition more generally evident between foreground and background in "Dutch" traditions, as in works by the elder Bruegel (for example, *Landscape with the Fall of Icarus* and *The Hunters in the Snow*), in which such divisions are managed diagonally, with the eye directed in the foreground to details clustered within the lower angle and in the upper angle toward the horizon and mountain peaks or open seas. In *The Professor's House,* such equilibrium (for the protagonist at least) is really a matter of memory; the foreground story of the novel is buried beneath a stuffy domesticity shucked only temporarily—when the Professor recalls Tom's mesa adventure—for "the fresh air that blew off the Blue Mesa" (Cather, *On Writing* 31–32). This lost equilibrium becomes evident in several places in the first book, "The Family," especially in the conclusion of the Professor's long reminiscence of Tom (occasioned by son-in-law Scott McGregor's doubts about Tom's reality):

> those first years, before Outland had done anything remarkable, were really the best of all. [St. Peter] liked to remember the charming groups of three he was always coming upon [Tom and St. Peter's daughters, Rosamond and Kathleen]. . . . Oh, there had been fine times in this old house then: family festivals and hospitalities, little girls dancing in and out, Augusta [the seamstress] coming and going, gay dresses hanging in his study at night, Christmas shopping and secrets and smothered laughter on the stairs. When a man had lovely children in his house, fragrant and happy, full of pretty fancies and generous impulses, why couldn't he keep them? (107)

Reminders of this lost equilibrium-giving life include the mixture of Augusta's patterns and the Professor's notes in the box couch and the comparison made between the Bayeux Tapestry and the Professor's best writing, the writing he produced when "he was conscious of pretty little girls in fresh dresses" in the house below and could interweave with "personal memories" the exploits of his Spanish adventurers (84–85).

Juggling roles as husband, father, teacher, and scholar (alternating them—cheating on one to serve another) had challenged St. Peter rather than posing a problem. Seeking the bachelor haven of the French garden and enjoying an epiphany off the coast of Spain without his wife represented his survival as a scholar; hardly blameworthy, such experiences helped maintain a creative balance between the absorbing domesticity of family life and the expansive historical vistas of scholarly exploration. The upsetting of this arrangement began after St. Peter, perceiving Tom as remarkable, took him up to his study and replaced his wife as his companion: "then Mrs. St. Peter withdrew her favour" (151). The destructive process continued as the Professor's daughters graduated from innocent play with Tom to competition for his favor. When the novel begins, Louie Marsellus is in Tom's skin and Mexican blanket as

Rosamond's husband, Kitty has married on the rebound, and the scene of domestic bliss (the old house) yawns emptily beneath the Professor's study. Lillian St. Peter makes an important point when warning her husband about the faulty gas heater in his study above the now-empty house: "It was very different when the house below was heated" (80). Although scholarship might generate its own heat, the scholar's (and artist's) protection against solipsistic annihilation is in the central heating of family life from which St. Peter has withdrawn.

The Professor himself has occasioned the loss of that balance between proximity and distance Cather appreciated in the Dutch paintings she saw in Paris, and the loss has led to creative sterility. Glass doorknobs, electric dinner buzzers, and painted Spanish bedroom sets (mere clutter where domestic life has failed) have obliterated the sunrise breaking over sculptured peaks and impassable mountains in Tom's country. Few readers question just what Godfrey St. Peter does during all those hours (including Christmas Day) he spends alone in his uncomfortable study. He seems forever sitting down to papers which, in the first chapter, he looks "musingly at" (10) until Augusta intrudes, and on Christmas he becomes engrossed in papers until lunch, when he pushes them aside to eat and reminisce about the convent girl to whom he offered dahlias during his student days in Paris. His confession to old Applehoff the landlord reveals St. Peter's actual activity: "I'm renting our house," he admits, "to have room to think" (41). This thinking is not toward the writing of histories; it is a futile effort to sustain a lost personal past, and the single project that might be classified as scholarly, the editing for publication of Tom's Blue Mesa diary ("a sketch of Outland . . . of his . . . many-sided mind, . . . simple and straightforward personality" [150]), is merely an attempt to resurrect Tom.

As the Professor withdraws because he cannot control his family the way he had before his wife withdrew and his daughters were adults, he is punished and exploited by that family. He is asked to help Kitty select her furs, Rosie her furniture; he vainly tries to revive the loving relationship his daughters once shared, vainly tries to keep his sons-in-law from damaging each other, vainly tries to instill in Rosamond a sense of responsibility for the Cranes and Augusta, and vainly tries to bridge the separation developing between himself and wife Lillian—taking up her glove at the opera and drawing it through his fingers before she turns away from him to survey the audience (78). He is not able to restore the best years through these efforts, and his recognition of that reality (an anticipation of the novel's final book) comes when he questions why one "couldn't . . . keep" one's "lovely children" in a house "full of pretty fancies and generous impulses" (107). Answering his question with a question, he wonders, "Was there no way but Medea's?" Thus, the fresh air that Cather and her Professor associate with Tom's mesa is effectively choked off by the domestic problems Cather stuffs into the first book; to compound this, the Professor's golden days of tracing the exploits of conquistadores have won him a prize and are gone. As he puts it, "the horse was gone—that was the thing he was feeling most just now" (22).

Despite his desperate efforts to keep them from disappearing, the distant peaks and seas associated with Tom have become increasingly difficult for St. Peter to remember. When Scott McGregor reveals that his classmate, Tom, "isn't very real to me any more. Sometimes I think he was just a—a glittering idea," St. Peter is "rather troubled" and begins "recalling as clearly and definitely as he could every incident of that . . . spring day . . . he first saw Tom Outland" (94–95). He, too, fears forgetting the romance of his life and in a subsequent scene begs Kitty to stay with him awhile to remember "that side of Tom" not "turned out chemicals and cents" (112). At the conclusion of St. Peter's conversation with Dr. Crane about patent money, the collapse of romance (the obliteration of those liberating upper diagonals and window scenes) is encapsulated in a passage at once recalling and undoing St. Peter's private epiphany off the coast of Spain:

> everything around [St. Peter] seemed insupportable, as the boat on which he is imprisoned seems to a sea-sick man. Yet it was possible that the little world, on its voyage among the stars, might become like that; a boat on which one could travel no longer, from which one could no longer look up and confront those bright rings or revolution. (131)

The obliteration terrifies the Professor, who stubbornly attempts to cling to the stars and whose domestic haven transforms into hell even as he resists its reality.

Denial of reality to sustain illusion is the crux of the final book and is what Cather referred to in her note on the novel to Robert Frost: "This is really a story of 'letting go with the heart' but most reviewers seem to consider it an attempt to popularize a system of philosophy" (Sergeant 215). The phrase "letting go with the heart" is from "Wild Grapes," which was published the year before *The Professor's House* in Frost's *New Hampshire* collection (1924). In it a female persona recalls being suspended in the air when picking grapes from a vine growing on a birch. When her brother releases the bent-down tree, she swings above the earth, dangling in fear yet too scared to drop. She compares letting go with the hands to letting go with the heart and mind; although each is a step in knowledge, an exploration of the frightening, she confesses never having to let go with the mind and hopes never to have to let go with the heart: "but nothing tells me / That I need learn to let go with the heart" (Frost 243). But Professor St. Peter must learn this painful process; it is demanded by time, age, and living. He can continue to live with his family, but the relationship must be altered, and Tom must recede into the past where he belongs. However, there is another meaning to "letting go with the heart," and that has to do with the novel's second problem cluster, referred to earlier as historical and cultural as well as social. It, too, requires the Professor's recognition that change is inevitable and that he must commit to values he merely praises in lip service.

The change St. Peter has resisted is the same that startles Henry Adams in *The Education* when he visits the Paris Exposition of 1900 under the guidance of American scientist Samuel Langley, who dismisses the entire art exhibit because of his obsession with the internal combustion engine and electric generator. The dynamo becomes for Adams the symbol of emerging industrial and technological society; juxtaposing the cross and the steam engine as forces, he is intrigued with the processes of production, respectively, of great cathedrals and dizzying generator wheels. Thus two kingdoms of force begin to divide history for him: that of the woman, a sexual force represented ultimately in the Virgin Mary, and that of the dynamo, a force propelling humanity toward atomic and nuclear discovery. In Cather's novel, a historian like Adams reluctantly confronts the realities of contemporary science: the Outland vacuum, the Outland engine revolutionizing aviation. Such realities have changed St. Peter's life; commercialized, they have corrupted both the St. Peter family and the university, turning the latter into a business school. Adams's dual kingdoms of force clarify the Professor's classroom comments on science as sterile, as stripping humanity of rich pleasure and diminishing human value: "I don't myself think much of science as a phase of human development," he begins. "It has given us a lot of ingenious toys; they take our attention away from the real problems. . . . As long as every man and woman who crowded into the cathedrals . . . was a principal in a gorgeous drama with God . . . life was a rich thing" (54–55). As jealousy over Tom's legacy grows into hatred between St. Peter's daughters, it becomes obvious that science's ingenious toys create debilitating problems, and the discord between the realms of force hinted at in the classroom becomes dramatically evident:

As the Angelus was ringing, two faces at once rose in the shadows . . . :

the handsome face of his older daughter . . . with cruel upper lip and scornful half-closed eyes . . . ; and Kathleen, her square little chin set so fiercely, her white cheeks actually becoming green under her swollen eyes. . . . He . . . went to his one window, . . . and stood looking at the dark clump of pine-trees . . . where the Physics building stood. A sharp pain clutched his heart. Was it for this the light in Outland's laboratory used to burn so far into the night! (74)

Here the laboratory and the Virgin, kingdoms of force which for Adams "had nothing in common but attraction" (1070), polarize, the former invading the latter, corrupting women who should represent it.

Like Adams, St. Peter is naive about the Virgin's force, a condition Adams identifies as the bankruptcy of his Yankee breeding, which equated woman and sex with sin and dismissed the Virgin as superstition. The Professor is similarly bankrupt; at Christmas, he asks Augusta if certain phrases from the Virgin's litany are in the "Magnificat," and then betrays astounding ignorance of that canticle, surprised that it is attributed to the Virgin in Luke's gospel. The attitude toward women bred into him he now almost identifies: Augusta has "brightened" his attic with her information about the Virgin as she had brightened all his holidays with feminine touches, and sometimes "she made those terrible women [the dress 'forms'] entirely plausible!" (84). The kind of study Adams undertakes at sixty-two to overcome the deficiencies in his education might be in store for Cather's Professor: "one stumbled," confesses Adams, "as stupidly [into the vast forests of scholastic science—from Zeno through Thomas Aquinas to Montaigne, Descartes, and Pascal] as though one were still a German student of 1860" (1075). Perhaps the Professor had already commenced such exploration (which might explain his questioning of Augusta), though it is still in its pagan infancy. Adams detects anticipation of the Virgin in the opening lines of Lucretius, where the poet invokes Venus "exactly" as Dante will invoke the Virgin: "thou alone dost govern the nature of things" (Adams 1071n4, 1244). St Peter recalls that Tom told his "story of youthful defeat" on one of those rainy nights in summer when "they sat inside and read Lucretius" (155).

To the extent that the Virgin's force in *The Professor's House* is represented in the "reliable, methodical . . . devout" (16) seamstress, Augusta, who drags him from his gas-filled study, St. Peter is saved from the dynamo by the Virgin. The change in him, so briefly sketched by Cather, is not merely a letting go with the heart as release; it is release for the purpose of loving universally (in the sense of charity) rather than privately. Godfrey St. Peter has been an emotionally niggardly and self-protective individual; lacking the generosity and public spiritedness of Louie Marsellus (58), he had depended on his wife's instincts "about what one owed to other people" (132). The "drawing-back that he feels in the region of his diaphragm" when Louie offers a summer in France (139) characterizes St. Peter's response to, among others, the Crane problem, to the feuding of his daughters, and to his wife's involvement with her sons-in-law. When complaining about Louie's florid style (36), he tells Lillian that he admires "reserve about one's deepest feelings"—the kind of reserve Tom exhibited for so long in burying the truth about his treatment of Roddy (155). Indeed, Tom, is admired for *lack* of public spirit by St. Peter right before the stove fails: "He couldn't see Tom building 'Outland,' or becoming a public-spirited citizen" (236). The denial of all such "realities" leads to the Professor's "falling out of all domestic and social relations, out of his place in the human family" (250). However, several pages after this impasse, he makes a distinction that separates the two kinds of letting go with the heart: "He didn't . . . feel any obligations toward his family. . . . [T]here was still Augusta, however; a world full of Augustas, with whom one was outward bound" (257).

Tom's Blue Mesa functions negatively and positively in the limited resolution of the Professor's story. It provides a reprieve from the novel's claustrophobic atmosphere but is qualified by diverting the Professor from the consequences of solipsism (reflected in Tom's treatment of Roddy). Also, it lacks significance culturally as merely a pre-Christian anticipation of the force that saves St. Peter. The mesa intrigues and tempts Tom like the Old Testament God; it blazes like fire and speaks in thunder (171–72). The ruined city within it is approached solemnly like a holy city "looking down into the canyon with the calmness of eternity" (180). Tom's Cliff City gives evidence of the integration of force and symbol that Adams attributes to the Virgin, but it is a dead, pagan city with a mummy goddess, an unredeemed Eve. Its living water, trickling from the rock "like liquid crystal . . . [throwing] off the sunlight like a diamond" (187), seems deficient in the restorative, sacramental powers found, say, in the ruined Euro-American settlement in Frost's "Directive," where the stream by the cedar is related to Christian baptism as well as the Eucharist and offers to modern humanity "whole[ness] again beyond confusion" (Frost 521). The mesa's limitation is also evident in Tom's temptation to keep his discovery of the city from Roddy as well as in the epiphany he eventually experiences at the cost of banishing his best friend and stifling the "ache in my arms to reach out and detain him" (223).

But the nature of Tom's epiphany is significant in its difference from Thea Kronborg's. Where hers is aesthetic, his is something more: "something had happened in me that made it possible for me to co-ordinate and simplify, and that process . . . brought with it great happiness. It was possession. . . . For me the mesa was no longer an adventure, but a religious emotion" (226–27). During his "possession," Tom complements the southwestern past with the European and then integrates them: "I got the better of the Spanish grammar and read the twelve books of the *Aeneid*. . . . When I look into the *Aeneid* now, I can always see two pictures: the one on the page, and another behind that: . . . little clustered houses . . . a rude tower . . . a dark grotto, in its depths a crystal spring" (227–28). However, Tom's accomplishments are constantly tempered by the memory of his rejection of Roddy: "I used to be frightened at my own heartlessness. . . . But the older I grow, the more I understand what it was I did that night on the mesa. Anyone who requites faith and friendship as I did, will have to pay for it" (228–29).

Cather has moved from aesthetic concerns to moral and religious concerns and from southwestern paganism to Judeo-Christian spirituality through European pre-Christian culture. Her alternatives to the mesa are suggested in the novel's final book, where (prior to his asphyxiation and recovery) St. Peter contemplates a summer trip and juxtaposes "the sculptured peaks and impassable mountain passes" of "Outland's country" and "Notre Dame, in Paris, . . . standing there like the Rock of Ages, with the frail generations breaking about its base" (246).

Epilogue

When Cather returned to Anasazi history in *Death Comes for the Archbishop* it was as a pretext for thoughts about God and Christianity. Riding past the Enchanted Mesa on his way to Ácoma, Latour reflects on concepts of the rock as "the utmost expression of human need" and as "the highest comparison of loyalty. . . . Christ Himself had used that comparison for the disciple [the original St. Peter] to whom he gave the keys of His Church" (97). The only ancient cliff dwellings in this southwestern novel are those in the Canyon de Chelly, believed by the Navajos to be the abodes of their gods, "inaccessible white houses set in caverns in the face of the cliffs" (292–93). The description, significantly, is sandwiched between those of mission churches: "the old warlike church of Ácoma, with its two stone towers[,] gaunt, grim, grey, . . . more like a fortress than a place of worship" (100); and the completed cathedral, as contemplated by the dying Archbishop ("good

Midi Romanesque of the plainest. . . . [H]ow it sounded the note of the South! . . . [T]he Cathedral lay against the pine-splashed slopes as against a curtain" [269]). The cultural straddling and fumbling religious musings in *The Professor's House* have been replaced by a conservative orthodoxy more objectionable even today than during the 1920s. When she was halfway through the *Archbishop*, Cather wrote to her agent at the time, Paul Reynolds, that her book concerns the French missionaries sent to New Mexico to bring order to the chaos of Indian, Spanish, and Mexican superstitions; she implies that, in effect, these Frenchmen extended the Kingdom by participating in creation. The "incompleteness" Latour notices in the physical landscape on his journey to Ácoma becomes symbolic of southwestern civilization; it is "as if, with all the materials . . . assembled, the Creator had desisted, gone away and left everything. . . . waiting to be made into a landscape" (94–95).

Conservative orthodoxy increases in Cather's next novel, *Shadows on the Rock*. Also, Professor St. Peter's speculation that "[a]rt and religion . . . are the same thing" (55) had been qualified by Myra Henshawe, who in *My Mortal Enemy* informs her confessor that "[r]eligion is different from everything else, because in religion seeking is finding" (77). When Cather accidentally discovered Quebec in 1928, she was inspired by a Frenchness (at the time more medieval than twentieth-century) essentially defined by religion, and in choosing the Counter-Reformation world of the seventeenth-century colony as her setting, she could mix French culture and Catholic belief in such a way that the former becomes the expression of the latter. The well-ordered universe of saints and martyrs illuminated by heavenly light and resembling a fresco (78) is duplicated sacramentally in the household order "[w]ithout [which], Madame Auclair tells her daughter, "our lives would be disgusting, like those of the poor savages. At home, in France," she continues, "we have learned to do all these things in the best way, and we are conscientious and that is why we are called the most civilized people in Europe and other nations envy us" (20). The "mountain rock" of Quebec, "cunningly built over with churches, convents, fortifications, gardens, following the natural irregularities of the headland on which they stood," resembles "nothing so much as one of those little artificial mountains . . . made in the churches [in France] to present the scene of the Nativity" (4). If Quebec is a new Bethlehem, it is more emphatically the New Jerusalem, "gleaming above the [St. Lawrence] river like an altar with many candles, or like a holy city in an old legend, shriven, sinless, washed in gold" (137). The comparison to the altar adds a layer of allusion, invoking, in addition to the Second Coming, the doctrine of transubstantiation, the changing of Eucharistic bread and wine into the physical presence of Jesus. The description also compresses several biblical passages and makes rock-set Quebec the transfigured church. In one of her early typescripts, Cather borrowed from Psalm 19:5 (all biblical references are to the King James version) to describe the sun as the "bridegroom issuing from his chamber," or the Lord emerging from his heavenly tabernacle to light the world, and used Matthew 13:43 (depicting the children of heaven shining at judgment like the sun) to compare the colonial community to "the righteous in their Heavenly Father's house." The entire passage owes to the transfigured city in Revelation 21, that of the tabernacle of the Lord adorned as a bride, generating its own light and descending to the righteous as their dwelling.

The genesis of Cather's holy city can be found in her 1902 travel sketches, where, in uncanny anticipation of Quebec, she describes "the fine old city of the popes," Avignon:

At the north end of the town there rises an enormous facade of smooth rock three hundred feet above the Rhone. This sheer precipice, accessible from the river side only by winding stone stairways, is crowned by the great palace of the popes. The palace is a huge, rambling Gothic pile, flanked by six square Italian towers, with a beautiful little cathedral in front. The palace faces toward the town, and behind it, overhanging the Rhone, are the popes' gardens. (Curtin 936–37)

In 1934, four years after the publication of *Shadows*, Cather returned to Avignon and decided to make it the locale of a story set during the exile of the popes, when the Roman Catholic Church was actually French. Edith Lewis provided George Kates with an account of the proposed plot, which involved the mutilation of two boys, Pierre and Andre, for thievery and blasphemy, respectively. The misery of their plight was to be heightened against the splendor of the papal court, and the central scene would involve an elderly, blind priest comforting the blasphemer. A major theme was to be an analysis of the betrayal of the sacred in the sinner, and the priest would succeed in transforming Andre's disability into a challenge involving Pierre (Kates 482–84). As to style, Lewis claimed that it was to be "completely démeublé" and the length of a long *nouvelle* (490), that is, like *My Mortal Enemy*. Avignon thus serves as a frame for forty-five years of fiction-writing rising from and returning to medieval European culture via excursions to the American Southwest and Northeast. Seen from this perspective, Thea Kronborg's eagle rising from the dwelling-peppered canyon as the embodiment of "[e]ndeavor, achievement, desire, glorious striving of human art!" (269) and Tom's city "looking down into the canyon with the calmness of eternity" (180) are merely transitional. More representative of the whole of Cather is the sentiment found in Isaiah 40:30–31: "Even the youth shall faint and be weary, and the young men shall utterly fail: but they that wait upon the Lord shall renew their strength; they shall mount up with wings as eagles; they shall run, and not be weary; *and* they shall walk, and not faint."

2. THE PROFESSOR'S HOUSE

Richard H. Millington

The Experience of Meaning in
The Professor's House

One sunny morning, on a street of comfortable, even grand old houses in Salt Lake City, a man—let's call him the Professor, because he is one—encounters a woman—let's call her Hillary, because that is her name. He is returning from walking his daughter to school, and the woman is a neighbor, one of a curiously vicarious sort, for the divorced Professor—his life perhaps representative of the fractured domesticities of his era—is just a visitor here. The desultory conversation turns, in the golden air, to the pleasures of the scenic, for these two bourgeois strangers will meet most comfortably on the common ground of taste and tourism. As the talk segues from the canyons of northern Utah to the rock formations of southern Utah, the Professor—his mind perhaps on a still-unwritten paper—mentions his own impending first encounter with the true Southwest, a conference at Mesa Verde. "Oh, Mesa Verde," says Hillary, "we were just there. It was so moving, it was one of the most moving experiences of my life!" After this moment of surprising intensity, the conversation loses steam, but Hillary—a nurse practitioner at a local clinic—ends it arrestingly: "Off to do pap smears!" It seemed to the Professor, as he wandered off, that he had just experienced *The Professor's House* in miniature: an assemblage of recognizable narrative elements—fractured domestic arrangements, human relationships mediated by the language of taste, even a middle-aged academic—interrupted, in their desultory unfolding, by a moment of stunning depth and meaning followed by an equally stunning lapse into inconsequence.

I take this little episode to indicate a problem of interpretation for readers of *The Professor's House*. There are many, many things to say about the novel, but, at least in my experience, it remains very hard to get at, because—as my anecdote implies—we are still so much inside the affective world it evokes, with its unmoored aestheticism, its voluble inconsequences, and its baffled authenticities. To put this problem in different, more recognizable scholarly terms: *The Professor's House* at once rewards and frustrates our current mode of interpretation because it supplies so *many* contexts: domesticity and the family; consumption; taste culture, collecting, and connoisseurship; the ruin; the museum; scholarship and the new university; and technology and the profit-system, not to mention the identity and psychological issues that unfold so richly within it. That is, it is already so astutely interested in the "institutions" of meaning—both established and emerging—that are central to twentieth-century American middle-class culture that no one context can persuasively occupy an explanatory center or sustain the relation of "depth" to the "surface" of the others. This essay is an attempt to work out a different interpretive tactic: What happens if we take the affective experience I tried to evoke in my opening tale as the book's primary historical datum, at once the object of its evocative powers and the focus of its analysis? What do we see if we place the experience of meaning itself at the center of our interpretive project? Here is the itinerary: I will begin by looking at what might be called the "meaning-structure" of the Professor's domestic life, finding there a pattern that defines the emergence of meaning throughout the novel's domestic scenes; I will then discuss "Tom Outland's Story," which, for all its interruptive force and aesthetic prestige, seems more to confirm this pattern than to disrupt it; and last I will consider the final section of the novel, tracking the Professor's actions as a kind of half-conscious reading of the shape of his own life and as a challenge for our own interpretation of the book.

Modernist Domesticity
In a brilliant reading of *The Scarlet Letter*, Lora Romero argued that the "modernism" of Hawthorne's novel—and, indeed, the prestige of the other American Renaissance texts we celebrate for their self-reflexive complexity—depends upon a particular cultural maneuver: the evocation of a "domesticity" that at once defines and establishes the superior seriousness, the fuller depth of the writer's (male) aesthetic (91–107). This has, by and large, been the way readers have interpreted the inner architecture of the Professor's house (even if they have reversed the values attached to the two domains): St. Peter's heroic scholarly career has been achieved by carving out of the household triviality a place of serious endeavor and by guarding the boundaries of that space

against all incursion and distraction. According to this view, his odd loyalty to his study expresses his fidelity to that higher life as against the feminized, commodity-filled life below.

But a closer look at the novel's first book (its title, "The Family," like that of the novel itself reminding us that this *is* a domestic novel) reveals something different and considerably more complex. The relation actually depicted between the study and the home, the Professor and the women of the family, is not exclusion but intermingling, not opposition but connection; his scholarly career is not threatened by but *depends upon* its proximity to the domestic. Hence the conjoined actions of the book's second sentence: "Professor St. Peter was alone in the dismantled house where he had lived ever since his marriage, where he had worked out his career *and* brought up his daughters" (3, my italics). Hence the mingling of documents—the Professor's research notes and Augusta's dress patterns—in the study/sewing room's archival upholstered box (13) and the Professor's affection for those inconvenient mannequins. Even as St. Peter describes his experience in the conventional language of separate spheres ("the sewing room . . . was the one place in the house where he could get isolation, insulation, from the engaging drama of domestic life" [16]), the book gives us a different, more symbiotic account of the Professor's creative life. Sitting atop the now-empty old house on Christmas morning, St. Peter remembers other Christmases:

> No matter how hard he was working, he had always felt the sense of holiday . . . steal up to his study from the house below. When he was writing his best, he was conscious of pretty little girls in fresh dresses— of flowers and greens in the comfortable, shabby sitting-room—of his wife's good looks and good taste. . . . All the while he had been working so fiercely at his eight big volumes, he was not insensible to the domestic drama that went on beneath him. (84–85)

Tellingly—for he is a man who writes in a sewing room—he compares his work to the double narrative of Queen Mathilde's tapestry, which surrounds the "big" male chronicle of the deeds of knights and heroes with what is identified as a woman's form, the "playful" doings of birds and beasts that compose "a story in themselves": "to him, the most important chapters of his history were interwoven with personal memories" (85). I am suggesting, then, that the Professor's battle for his study expresses less his nostalgia for his brilliant, self-isolating career than his half-conscious fidelity to the mixed and intermingled form of meaning that has unfolded within it, an experience we might call, adapting Romero, modernist domesticity. It is as if Cather has analyzed the modernist fantasy that Romero identifies and uses one of its apparent exemplars—St. Peter the patriarch-intellectual—to take it apart. But Cather's interests here extend beyond such ironies, and I want to argue more broadly that the key element in her complex portrayal of the Professor's domestic life early in the novel is her identification of the "shape" or "structure" of meaning within that life, and that the pattern she identifies at the book's beginning—of an apparently hierarchical opposition that turns out to be a generative juxtaposition—characterizes the experience of meaning in the book more largely and comes to constitute its theory of the meaningful: its enactment and analysis of the affective life of this precinct of American modernist culture.

Meanings in Circulation

When one looks at the representation of the emergence or loss of meaning within *The Professor's House*, it seems to follow the pattern we have begun to observe. Just as the creativity of St. Peter's writing is redescribed as an effect of the intermingling or "proximity" of scholarship and domesticity, so the book's other moments of most intense significance seem to follow a "horizontal" principle or strategy of production: "next-to-ness," or displacement, or "recycling," or borrowing. One might think here of Lillian transferring her erotic energies to flirtation with her sons-in-law. Or of the many ways the term "Outland" circulates within the text: as patent, as profit, as the name of Louie and Rosamond's new estate, or, conversely, as the marker of values not bounded by the marketplace. Such a pattern of surprising sequencings, or depths that surface on the wing of a juxtaposition, seems to govern the text's account of the emotional life of its characters. For example, the frankest, most generous mutual acknowledgment of the emptiness of Lillian and Godfrey's marriage comes and goes in a moment, touched off by chance and memory, at a performance of *Mignon* (78); the most affectionate moment we witness between Scott and Kitty recalls an earlier confession of *her* love for Tom, and the bond between them is expressed as an acknowledgment of this shared knowledge; the Professor's beautiful evocation, in memory, of his family's household bliss in the years before Tom's successes yields a stunning, utterly convincing reversal of parental sentiment: "When a man had lovely children in his house, fragrant and happy, full of pretty fancies and generous impulses, why couldn't he keep them? Was there no way but Medea's, he wondered?" (107). A perhaps trivial—but for me convincing—sign of these operations of signification is the novel's epigraph, which is not, as is customary, a line or two imported from another literary work but a sentence belonging to Louie Marsellus, curiously recycled from within the text as though to remind us that, in this novelistic world, meanings are an effect of circulation rather than an artifact of a preexisting, authoritative scheme.

It is, I think, through the figure of Louie Marsellus that we most fully see this meaning-structure in operation and might best appreciate its interpretive implications. In many readings of the novel, Marsellus appears as a transparent figure, the avatar supreme of the final triumph of commodity culture the book deplores, converting Tom's bones into a "personal asset," aesthetic response into connoisseurship, and intellectual inquiry into profit. I suppose all of this is true, but he also—and it is this "also-ness" that defines the book's vision of meaning—produces the book's sole moment of unmixed ethical heroism, and he achieves that heroism not by exorcising or transcending the commercial values he espouses but through an occasion they provide. I am thinking of the scene during which the Professor witnesses Louie's response to Rosamond's revelation that Scott had blackballed Louie from the Arts and Letters Club, an action as full of her anger at Louie's generosity as it is resentful of Scott's prejudice. Between Rosamond's grasping rage and Scott's pettiness, the Professor is moved to apologize to Louie for his family. Louie's forgiveness of Scott is admirable enough, but his remarks on Rosamond are stunning: "I love her when she's naughty. She's a bit unreasonable sometimes, but I'm always hoping for a period of utter, of fantastic unreasonableness, which will be the beginning of a great happiness for us all" (149). "Louie, you are magnanimous and magnificent!" says the Professor. The magnanimity is easy to see, but the particular quality of the "magnificence" is harder to describe. What strikes me is not only the beautiful surprise of Louie's own "unreasonableness," which fractures the notion that his function is to play surface to the Professor's or Tom's depth, but also the curiously circumstantial or merely sequential quality of both this moment of heroism and of Louie's hopes for Rosamond. He puts his faith not in growth or reform—a depth model of character—but in surprise, a kind of sequencing. He reminds us that, for all the book's hostility toward commercial culture, its moments of fullest value depend not upon a hierarchy of depth and surface but upon the unpredictable effects of placement. (Indeed, in the moral world of the book, most of the cruelty is created by a mistaken application of a theory of depths, as when Rosamond and Kathleen make commodities—which for the entrepreneurial Louie are merely expressers of a circulating pleasure— carry their envy and rage.) In *The Professor's House* meanings are cut loose from any overarching or undergirding, romantic or religious, structure, but such moments—episodic, juxtapositional, inconsequent—are no less full for floating free.

The Lure of the Authentic

The most serious threat to my account of *The Professor's House* is, of course, "Tom Outland's Story." While the formal relation between this *nouvelle* and the domestic novel that surrounds it might seem to exemplify the "juxtapositional" pattern I have been describing, its apparent effect on our reading is quite different. "Tom Outland's Story," which, in Cather's well-known image, blows through the assembled proprieties and commodities of the rest of the book like "the fresh air that blew off the Blue Mesa" (*On Writing* 31–32), seems to trumpet its superior authenticity, its transcendent depth. Where the domestic novel gives us mere connoisseurship, Tom's story provides an intense experience of aesthetic unity; where the Professor's house features domestic anomie, the mesa supplies us with a set of imaginary ancestors and a community of faithful workers in the kingdom of art, or at least archaeology; where this wilderness tale evokes a kind of anthropological version of sacredness, the bourgeois novel goes shopping. Yet if "Tom Outland's Story" is a window, it is also a mirror, and meaning in that narrative, for all its absorbing authority, is also an effect of displacements and substitutions. In saying this, I am not attempting to reveal a secret emptiness at the core of Tom's narrative (even though the outcomes of both the domestic and the "adventure" narratives are, from a certain point of view, the same: many goods pass duty-free through the City of Mexico). Rather, my claim is that its fullnesses and emptinesses, for all the apparatus of authenticity, are like those of the novel that surrounds it: the effects of juxtaposition and surprise rather than the upswellings of an essential authenticity.

The best way to see this is late in Tom's story, as his narrative acknowledges the fragmentation of his dream. The sequence I have in mind begins with the now famous, or infamous, claim of ancestry—"I'm not so poor that I have to sell the pots and pans that belonged to my poor grandmothers a thousand years ago" (219)—which Tom uses, at least in part, to guilt-trip Roddy Blake. I think Charles Crow is right, in his recent essay on museum theory and *The Professor's House*, to see this claim both as overblown and as *known* to be overblown by the older Tom, who tells this story and admits to lying to enhance the effect of his wounded piety (56). But for my purposes, what is so interesting about the conjunction of Roddy's betrayal and Tom's outrage is the *number* of meanings, of perspectives, of narrative possibilities that follow, in surprising sequence, from it. First, there is Roddy's forceful, class-based critique of the economics of Tom's filial piety: "But I see now I was working for you like a hired man, and while you were away I sold your property" (222). Following that—but in a relation of addition, not refutation—is Tom's discovery that the loss of the artifacts has paradoxically enhanced his response to the mesa, yielding an experience of aesthetic possession and happiness much more powerful than his grandiose sense of loss: "This was the first time I ever saw it as a whole" (226). Yet this "high art" moment, an experience of cultural reverence apparently purged of the commodity-logic so prevalent in the novel, yields, with no implication of irony or demystification, to a no less powerful but profoundly different ethical perception: "the older I grow, the more I understand what it was I did that night on the mesa. Anyone who requites faith and friendship as I did will have to pay for it" (229). Finally, and in a curious way, Roddy himself—not the artifacts he has sold on Tom's behalf—becomes the precious lost object of the narrative's yearning, the object of its searches and of the curiosity of its hearers. Like Crow's argument, the interpretation I am pursuing here (along with the "reclamation" of Louie Marsellus I suggest above) implies a local challenge to the overarching claim made in Walter Benn Michaels's influential essay "The Vanishing American" that Cather is unwittingly in the grip of a widely shared fantasy of Indian ancestry that turns "culture" into a version of the racialism it appeared to contest in 1920s America. What we witness as this scene unfolds is not the emergence of a single, underlying master trope that structures the narrative and the social world to which it refers—as though an allegory buried in the cultural imagination had just surfaced—but a proliferation of meanings that offer competing accounts of the emotional and ethical weight of this moment of loss and gain.

"Tom Outland's Story," which seems so eccentric to the rest of the book, is, I am arguing, quite characteristic. Though it seems to purvey itself as a locus of the authentic within the book (a resonant archaeological depth to a trivial, commercialized surface), meaning within this narrative, no less than in the novel proper, is episodic, juxtapositional, circulatory: sequential, not consequential. Indeed, it is the younger Tom's fidelity to an overly simple narrative of depth, of a singular authenticity—"There was an ache in my arms to reach out and detain him, but there was something else that made me absolutely powerless to do so" (223)—that drives him during his single-minded attack on Roddy, thwarting love's expressive ache.

The Professor's Story

As they reinscribe St. Peter as the reader of this tale, the last words of "Tom Outland's Story"—"the rest you know"—invite us to interpret the last book of the novel as the Professor's response to Tom's story. For us, it is simultaneously a chance to ask what kind of ending is available to books more invested in circulation than teleology. Perhaps it would be best to end with a simple, fundamental juxtaposition in the Ecclesiastes mode: the Professor's story shows us that there is a time for family and a time for solitude, a time for creativity and a time for nostalgia. But it seems to me that Cather's farewell to the Professor is too insistently composed—too witty, if that is the word—in its relation to what has gone before for us to close out our interpretation so resoundingly.

In several ways, the sequence of thoughts that lead the Professor so close to suicide reflects his encounter with Tom's story. For instance, his meditation on the role of chance in his life is provoked by the illogic of Tom's death, and his sense that an early death might enhance a life's meaning is produced by thinking that Tom's unlooked-for demise saved him from an inevitable decline into quotidian trivialities. The trajectory of St. Peter's later life seems to replay Tom's story, but for him the alluring embodiment of the authentic is not a set of tribal ancestors but a primitive within, a lost boyhood self. If for Tom the temptation of the authentic led to his repudiation of Roddy, St. Peter's attraction to this deep, static, declarative earlier self leads toward death: "But now he thought of eternal solitude with gratefulness; as a release from every obligation, from every form of effort. It was the Truth" (248). But St. Peter is rescued from the final authenticity by an agent of the circumstantial. When Augusta pulls St. Peter from his toxic study, we might merely see the operations of chance, but the narrative makes it clear that what really saves St. Peter, what returns him to "the world of men and women," is the instructive proximity of her way of life to his: "If he had thought of Augusta sooner, he would have got up from the couch sooner. Her image would have at once suggested the proper action" (255). And, a little later in the text, "There was still Augusta, however; a world full of Augustas, with whom one was outward bound" (257). His encounter with Augusta, this is to say, has not so much refuted his despair as restored him to circulation, to the fullness and emptiness of a livable inconsequence.

I do not imagine that the view I have offered here captures the full range of the novel's interests or its complex relation to the middle-class culture of the early twentieth century that it describes and addresses. But to focus our attention on the book's surprising description of the meaning-life of its characters permits us, I think, to see in a new way Cather's own historicism and her place within the literary history of American modernism. For what *The Professor's House* offers us is a history, at the point of its emergence, of the affective life of what is still, from the liberal arts college to the *New Yorker*, our established culture, our culture of record—a history that is perhaps so hard to read because it is still so close to home.

Merrill Maguire Skaggs

Cather and the Father of History

One fact that, like a disreputable neighbor, we have seen but not known for decades is that Willa Cather was friendly with Mark Twain. Not only did she point out that she had loved and attentively read *Tom Sawyer*, to which she refers in *The Professor's House* (Professor St. Peter's colleague "Lily" Langtry gives students credit in history for reading *Tom Sawyer* [55]), but she also considered *Adventures of Huckleberry Finn* one of the three enduring American classics (Woodress 182). In May 1897 Cather wrote in the *Home Monthly*, "I got a letter last week from a little boy just half-past seven who had just read 'Huckleberry Finn' and 'Tom Sawyer.' He said, 'If there are any more books like them in the world, send them to me quick.' I had humbly to confess to him that if there were any others, I had not the good fortune to know of them." Cather adds, "I would rather sail on the raft down the Missouri with 'Huck' Finn and Jim than go down the Nile in December or see Venice from a gondola in May" (O'Brien, *Stories* 890–91).

She also knew Twain the man. At the 1998 Cather colloquium at Drew, Robert Comeau surveyed these acknowledged facts in order to prod the question, "Knew Twain how well?" As Comeau reminded us, Cather was present at Twain's seventieth birthday party for 150 friends and was also among those select 50 guests who enjoyed pre-dinner conversation with the guest of honor. This fact is arresting when we recall that Twain's birthday party at Delmonico's occurred in 1905—that is, in the year *before* Cather moved to New York to work at *McClure's*. As Comeau pointed out, Cather knew Twain well enough in New York to describe him as an "old lion in bed telling stories" (Woodress 210), storytelling sessions at which she was apparently present as a listener and eyewitness. She knew Twain pretty well, we gather.

In 1905 Cather was an ambitious young writer, full of curiosity and aware of the usefulness of a powerful literary sponsor. We would expect her, in the nature of things, to have jumped at a chance to closely observe or converse with Twain, because at that time he was probably the most famous man on earth. And by 1905 Twain was certainly accustomed to being watched, listened to, and appreciated. But we are still uncertain about how well Twain thought he knew, or was even aware of, the then-uncelebrated Miss Cather. He knew her well enough to invite her into his bedside entourage, of course. We also know that he admired her poem "The Palatine," which appeared in *McClure's* in June 1909, and read it out loud to Albert Bigelow Paine with enough gusto that Paine reprinted three verses of the poem in the third volume of his Twain biography (Woodress 210). We know that after his wife died in 1904 Twain had an eye for pubescent girls, but we also know that in 1905 Cather was not exactly dewy, since she was in her early thirties. So we must assume that the mature, if still spritely, Willa impressed that old lion by her personality, her individuality, and her character.

They must have talked. After she had told him of her intense admiration for his boys' adventures, already articulated for *Home Monthly* in 1897, they had for conversation the work each was doing at the time. Twain was writing increasingly "shocking" comments in a variety of forms on "the damned human race." Because Cather was just starting to make her reputation, she may have been somewhat modest, though she certainly had ample work to describe. But Twain was never diffident, and what was on his mind were final statements: the fragments and papers he had been jotting intermittently since the 1870s and was publishing during 1905 and 1906 under such titles as *Extracts from Adam's Diary* (1893, 1903, 1906) and *Eve's Diary* (1906). He was throwing off fragments in the form of diaries, soliloquies, and journal entries written by various members of the first family—not just Adam and Eve but also several of their descendants. Many of these fragments, however, were not published until 1962, when Bernard DeVoto gathered them together and called them "Papers of the Adam Family." Yet many of these fragments have at least a tangential relation to Cather's Mother Eve in *The Professor's House*, since falls from paradise become a theme as soon as such names or characters appear. The group of Adam papers as a whole, however, does not seem any more influential on *The Professor's House* than other current works—say *The Education of Henry Adams*'s puns on the Adams family history since time began.

In skimming through Twain's Adam Family fragments, we can certainly find small correspondences that seem to belong in the same neighborhood as Cather's Mother Eve or her Professor of European history. For example, Twain's Adam thinks Sunday is hellish and jots in his diary of a Sunday, "pulled through" (*Collected Tales* 99), while Cather's Professor takes a diabolical Sunday journey before which he refuses to communicate with his wife and during which he avoids his work, maliciously teases his landlord, and tempts his colleague Langtry. A word Twain's Adam quickly uses as a weapon is "justification" (*Collected Tales* 101)—just what Godfrey demands Augusta provide for the practices of the church. Twain's Adam insists "that principles have no real force except when one is well fed" (102), so he eats Eve's apples, while Cather's St. Peter requires a choice Christmas Day lunch that includes chicken sandwiches, grapes, and two perfect pears. Twain's snake suggests that the best way to get an education is to eat forbidden fruit (101), while Cather's St. Peter dishes out forbidden ideas to his students under the guise of educating them, ideas the Methodists somehow let him get away with. Twain's Eve brings death into the world and thus saves wild carnivores who can now eat each other (102); Cather's Outland shoots wild cows and eats them himself. Twain's Eve expresses the *joy* of being alive in Eden, though the land outside provides grief (707); St. Peter faces his own eviction from innocent delight when he anticipates a future outward bound with Augusta. Twain makes Cain red-haired like himself (105) and then proceeds to raise Cain; Cather's Professor raises more than a modicum of Cain himself, by design.

But these are small coincidences that fail to stop the breath or startle the pulse. Toward the end of DeVoto's "Papers of the Adam Family," however, we hit a three-fragment sequence that changes those rhythms. At the beginning of the trio DeVoto writes that the sequence caused "the translator [that is, Twain himself] much trouble which his editor was to repeat after him" (92). In explaining Twain's unpublished fragments, which DeVoto calls "translations," DeVoto adds,

> I have had to piece these translations together from a variety of manu-
> scripts, fragmentary, half-deleted, partly revised, with few clues to the
> order that Mark Twain intended them to have. I have arranged them
> in what seems to me a proper sequence, in a sequence which at least
> progressively describes the chaos of society. I cannot date any of the
> manuscripts but I think that they were all written in 1906. (92–93)

What follows at this point, when the Adam Family papers are well under way, is a triplet of fragments that seems to me directly related to *The Professor's*

House. The Twain who wrote them around 1906 is calling himself many things, among them "The Father of History," "The Bishop of New Jersey," and "The Mad Philosopher, Reginald Selkirk." Unless Twain gave her copies, how would Cather have seen these pages? And why would she recall this *particular* sequence—that is, assuming it was given to her—when she started designing *The Professor's House*?

A triggering event for pulling them out may have been the publication of Twain's "Eve Speaks" and "Adam's Soliloquy" in 1923, just as Cather started working up Professor St. Peter. But what she would reach for to review, I believe, starts with this passage in a scrap labeled "From the Diary of a Lady of the Blood, Third Grade." To see it as clearly as necessary, one needs remember only that "you little rat" was Twain's fondest term of endearment in the last decade of his life and that "Washoe" had been his marker for himself since 1864 (Quirk 8):

> She was a lovely little rat, and sweetly captivating: slender, lissome, brown-eyed, dimpled, complexioned like a peach blossom, frisky, frol-icsome, graceful—just a picture, she was, just a poem. She was of foreign extraction; her little drop of nobility had trickled down to her, in the lapse of time, from a great lord whose habitat was in a remote land many meridians of longitude away, the Duke of Washoe. He was descended from me [the female diarist] through—I forget the name, now—but the source was my daughter Regina's branch, I mean the one proceeding from Regina's second marriage. He was second cousin to—but I have forgotten that name, too. The little bride's name was Red Cloud, and was as foreign as her extraction. It was a kind of inheritance. (DeVoto 90)

Some may not think this rambling segment provides a strong enough signal for us to assume that Twain was writing with Willa Cather from Red Cloud in mind or that in it he was telling her, "we're alike, you and me, *because* we're different from the rest, and you belong to my foreign and noble bloodline—the old Adam bloodline." What each one thinks is personal business. But what *Cather* thought when she read, as she must have read, this meandering, I think we can know. I think she thought she was being addressed directly here, because virtually every phrase and detail that follows, in Twain's three subsequent fragments, finds a clear echo, or repetition and inclusion, in *The Professor's House*. In her 1925 novel Cather is deliberately recycling material in order to be in *direct* dialog with Twain, and he started this conversation.

In this triptych of "translations," Twain gives us two men, one an older professor and the other a young genius. The royal lady whose diary we first read calls that older man "the Mad Prophet," though we are told that "he merely builds prognostications, not prophecies . . . builds them out of history and statistics, using the facts of the past to forecast the probabilities of the future. It is merely applied science" (DeVoto 93). My point is that Godfrey St. Peter of *The Professor's House* has two parents—Mark Twain and Willa Cather—who together create in him their son, the child of their imaginations. (We may recall that St. Peter's sons—those children which are his books— are born, as Louie Marcellus remarks, in the third-floor attic [165].) Both of these engendering parents, Twain and Cather, are engaged in ruminations about history, the nature of civilization, and the probable course of the future. But the coupling as well as the splitting of characters into two parts begins with Twain's loving couple—the Godfrey and Lillian St. Peter equivalents. The Twain diarist goes on, "I have known the Mad Prophet—or the Mad Philosopher, . . . ever since he was a student in college. . . . He was nineteen or twenty then. I have always had a kindly feeling for him; partly, of course, because of the good qualities of his head and heart." We recall that Cather says of her young lovers, "they had been young people with good qualities, and very much in love"(257). We also remember that St. Peter had a romance of the heart and of the mind or imagination (258). Twain's diarist similarly summarizes, "He married when he was twenty-four, and when neither he nor the girl was properly situated to marry, for they were poor" (93). Twain adds, "they were an impatient little pair and dreadfully in love with each other" (94).

Here we note three coincidences. First, this description matches St. Peter's memories of his student days, when he met Lillian at age twenty-four and felt they "must marry" (49). Second, Cather was twenty-four in the year 1898–99, when she became involved with Isabelle McClung. As readers, we register that Twain understood twenty-four as the age of defining romance and that he acknowledges here a two-part unit composed of a male professor side and a female Red Cloud side, an "impatient little pair." Third, Cather chooses to underscore in her novel the significant twenty-fourth year and its romance *after* Twain has acknowledged it.

The Twain sketch, with the Lady of the Blood speaking, continues: "My influence got the lad a small mathematics professorship in his university" (we recall that Tom Outland, initially uninstructed in mathematics, learns it quickly in one summer of focused work [121]). Twain's lady continues, "and he worked hard. . . . The couple remained poor, and are poor yet, but as happy as many that are richer. They have always had enough for their needs, for my influence has kept him in his post, and has also augmented his salary a little, more than once" (94). In Cather's version of this fiction, alumni from St. Peter's classes had to use their influence to keep his job available to him when Langtry's influential relative tried to get it from him (55), and the small inheritance from her father keeps Lillian St. Peter in good spirits (29).

What triggers Twain's diary fragment, however, are the mad professor's comments on a new force invented by "the amazing man called 'The Prodigy,' who rose out of obscurity in the middle of the fifth century and in a few years conquered the world" through "the wonderful new force, liquefied thought" (95, 94). At this point we hail not only Tom Outland's prototype but also Tom's invention, which Cather describes in *The Professor's House* as both vacuum and gas (40, 61). That almost unparalleled Catherian inconsistency may be a private joke she shares with Twain about the nature of human thought: whether it is liquefied or not, it is still either vacuum or gas. Readers recall that Tom's discovery becomes a "bulkheaded vacuum revolutionizing aviation" (40). Twain's diary fragment explains,

> Before he came, today, the Philosopher had been examining the mobile which is propelled by the wonderful new force, liquefied thought. . . .
> He said he could see no reason why this force should not displace steam and electricity, since it is much more powerful than those agents, occupies almost no space, and costs next to nothing. That is, the cost to the Trust that owns the patent is next to nothing. It is the same Trust that owns the globe's railways and ships—the globe's transportation, in a word. (94–95)

The patent, of course, is the key in *both* stories. It is the patent that Louie Marcellus has exploited so successfully. And where did Twain's Prodigy get the inspiration for his new force? Twain tells us:

> I am of the opinion that the development of this mysterious new force has not yet proceeded beyond the infancy stage. I think we know but little about it now, compared with what we shall know a few decades hence. Why it may turn out to be the renowned and lamented Lost Force of old tradition! And it isn't mere tradition; there is history for it. . . . You know the tradition yourself . . . like the rest of the world—but you do not know the history. It has just been deciphered from the clay archives of an exhumed city of the Double Continent; and when it is published the nations will perceive that . . . the amazing man called "the Prodigy," who rose out of obscurity . . . and conquered the world[,] . . .

subdued the rest of the globe without spilling blood, except in a single instance. (95–96)

Cather's single instance of bloodletting occurs when Henry is struck by a rattlesnake.

By now some readers may have remembered fair Rosamond with the lavender moleskin complexion, so like "a little rat." For that matter, we may have recalled Lillian's "pink and white complexion" (58), which suggests "a real peach blossom." We may have recalled the marital history of the St. Peters, kept happy until its later days by Lillian's extra income. We may acknowledge that the world Tom triumphantly possessed was Cliff City, which he exhumed and whose artifacts he tried to decipher. Before leaving Twain's first three pages, however, we can spot a prototype for Dr. Crane and a pattern for Tom's death. Twain's prodigy has actually come into possession of his force by correctly deciphering work of "one Napeer, an obscure person" who discovered and then tried to destroy "his secret, since war was already terrible enough." But the shoemaker-emperor who is the Prodigy studied the papers of Napeer and deduced that secret. "He found the formula, mastered its details, then destroyed it. . . . [T]hen, by accident, he blew himself up with his machine . . . and his formidable secret died with him" (96). This fragment ends as the philosopher/polymath/historian is just beginning to discuss his Law of Periodical Repetition and its corollary, the Law of the Permanency of the Intellectual Average (97).

Two more fragments succeed this pivotal one in DeVoto's collection and seem to me worthy of consideration by Cather scholars. Immediately following the "Diary of the Lady of the Blood" is an "Extract from the Discourse of Reginald Selkirk, the mad Philosopher, to her grandeur, the Acting Head of the Human Race." The title tells the most important point: Twain's "acting head of the human race" is Mother Eve. She listens to the rhetorical question posed by the Mad Philosopher: "What is a civilization, rightly considered?" This is the central question of all three parts of *The Professor's House*. Twain's Mad Philosopher pretty well sums up the point of view put forth by both Cather and Twain:

> Our civilization is wonderful, in certain spectacular and meretricious ways; wonderful in scientific marvels and inventive miracles; wonderful in material inflation, which it calls advancement, progress, and other pet names; wonderful in its spying-out of the deep secrets of Nature and its vanquishment of her stubborn laws; wonderful in its extraordinary financial and commercial achievements; wonderful in its hunger for

money, and in its indifference as to how it is acquired; wonderful in
the hitherto undreamed-of magnitude of its private fortunes and the
prodigal fashion in which they are given away. (97)

Past the shared concerns we find in Twain's and Cather's fictions, however,
are two equally arresting differences this second fragment highlights: Twain's
philosopher addresses Eve as "Her Grandeur." Cather's Eve, conversely, is not
grand but merely dead; she is what remains of a sexual victim in a sexist world,
who falls out of sight screaming. Twain's fragments pay a gallant's tribute to
female power of various kinds; Twain's women are royal and grand, supremely
powerful, and literate—the writers and keepers of the word. Cather's Eve
is a sardonic comment on Twain's version of female power, for his Eve is
"acting head of the human race." Cather's Eve cannot act, being only a
mummy, and her female forms are headless: either they are women the
Professor decides are empty-headed or else they are headless ideas. Either
Cather is more misogynist than Twain or her 1925 view of Western history,
being more consistent than Twain's, is infinitely blacker than his was even
in his last, blackest decade. Her novel, in my opinion, is the most stunningly
comprehensive indictment of patriarchal Western civilization ever coherently
crafted in fiction by an American. At the least, it is not merely "a grim, nasty
little tale" (Woodress 367).

Twain's third fragment in the sequence we are focusing on is called "Passage
from a Lecture." In it a "distinguished Professor of the Science of Historical
Forecast" discusses the two laws of Reginal Selkirk, the Mad Philosopher.
The Law of Periodical Repetition explains that history not only repeats itself
but that "nature has no originality" (99). Thus, not only does the average
stay the same, but even the exceptions, such as the Prodigy or Tom Outland,
are predictably repeated at regular intervals. So, the lecturer asks, "Will this
wonderful civilization of today perish?" He then answers, "Yes, everything
perishes. Will it rise and exist again? It will—for nothing can happen that
will not happen again. And again, and still again, forever" (101). An empty
Cliff City becomes an image for such periodical repetition in Cather. Not
surprisingly, talk of suicide in Twain precedes talk of his law, since living
seems "too much trouble, unless one can get something big out of it," not
mere repetition, as Thea Kronborg pointed out in *The Song of the Lark* (219).

What can we see, then, we ask along with Professor St. Peter, when
the cycles we anticipate ahead of us seem so devoid of delight? A Twain
ventriloquist doubles back to answer:

By the Law of Periodical Repetition, everything which has happened once must happen again and again and again—and not capriciously, but at regular periods, and each thing in its own period, not another's, and each obeying its own law. The eclipse of the sun, the occultation of Venus, the arrival and departure of the comets, the annual shower of stars—all these things hint to us that the same Nature which delights in periodical repetition in the skies is the Nature which orders the affairs of the earth. Let us not underrate the value of that hint. (100)

So what shall we do with this material? We cannot prove beyond the shadow of a doubt that Twain designed his little handmade valentine for Cather, a card from an old man in high spirits to a young woman who seemed a real peach blossom. We cannot prove that he gave her copies of the fragments, nor that Cather had these Twain materials in hand when she wrote *The Professor's House*. But if we choose to ignore this most likely explanation for the correspondences between these texts, we only confirm Twain's Law of Periodical Repetition, while we reduce Cather to a paper cutout in a chain of writer dolls. If we choose to ignore Twain's scraps, we must either assume that he corrupted her terribly, that she festered twenty years and then erupted, or else that she was so starstruck she remembered scraps of his conversation *exactly*, after which *both* writers went somewhere at some time and separately replicated those conversational moments verbatim, but exactly the same way.

Personally, I would rather believe that both Twain's scraps and *The Professor's House* are more important than that. I believe that Cather's novel is a masterpiece whose impact stems from Cather's willingness to face unblinkingly the appalling implications of ideas Twain preferred to make (admittedly amusing) jokes about. Unlike Cather, Twain blinked a little, at least when it came to some women he liked. Because I believe Twain to be a profoundly great writer, flippant or not, I am deeply gratified to observe these signs of his insight in recognizing Cather's importance. As Oliver Wendell Holmes said to James Russell Lowell at the end of a four-hour dinner with young William Dean Howells, "Well, James, this is something like the apostolic succession; this is the laying on of hands" (Brooks et al. 1344).

Tom Quirk

Twain and Cather, Once Again

Merrill M. Skaggs's essay, "Cather and the Father of History," explores in provocative detail a possible and possibly important connection between Willa Cather and Mark Twain and in doing so moves us closer to a clearer and more definite sense of that relationship. My own previous exploration of this subject, in *Coming to Grips with "Huckleberry Finn,"* was much fuzzier. Still, at the time, I was attempting to make more discernible, and therefore more palpable, the influence that Twain might have exerted upon a writer I believed was one of his literary heirs.

Skaggs, by contrast, means to navigate trickier waters, for she is dealing not merely with influences but with sources as well. The differences between the two are important. The study of influences is impressionistic, perhaps fanciful; the study of sources is largely a factual inquiry. And we now know, due to the efforts made by the editors of the Cather scholarly editions project, that Cather used sources far more extensively and frequently than was previously supposed. What is more, source study often provides access to the deeper recesses of an author's imagination. While much of what Skaggs has to say cannot be absolutely proved, her essay nonetheless opens up specific avenues of inquiry that influence study alone could never do.

Before examining some of the more interesting features of her essay, I want to observe that we both are implicitly suggesting that at some point Cather began to think of herself as a western writer. I doubt I would have ever recognized this as an aspect of my own intent without Skaggs's investigation. Still, the vernacular point of view that I believed Cather derived from Twain's example is essentially a western one. Cather is eloquent on this point in her 1922 preface to *Alexander's Bridge* (1912) in which she dismisses her first novel in favor of her second novel, *O Pioneers!* (1913), the latter being the stimulating example of dealing with her native Nebraska and "hitting the home pasture." Such a satisfying work results, she said, when a writer's "life line'" and "the line of his personal endeavor meet" (preface vi).

Cather returned to the same subject in 1931 in "My First Novels (There Were Two)," but there she made interesting refinements in her argument. For one thing, the "home pasture" has gained considerably in its extent. No longer is her attachment to familiar literary material confined exclusively to the plains. Shortly after finishing *Alexander's Bridge*, Cather wrote, "I went for six months to Arizona and New Mexico. The longer I stayed in a country I really did care about, and among people who were a part of the country, the more unnecessary and superficial a book like *Alexander's Bridge* seemed to me" (*On Writing* 92). The desert Southwest cured her of the "editorial point of view" and the (largely commercial) desire to create drawing-room characters chatting about interesting things. In the same essay, she curiously refers to her childhood home in Nebraska as a "ranch," not a farm. Perhaps even more significantly, she recalls her separation from the eastern writers she once tried to emulate: "But Henry James and Mrs Wharton were our most interesting novelists, and most of the younger writers followed their manner, without having their qualifications" (93).

Then there is the preface to *The Best Stories of Sarah Orne Jewett* (1925), in which she names the three "masterpieces" of American fiction—*The Scarlet Letter*, *Huckleberry Finn*, and *The Country of the Pointed Firs*. Since this essay was the first thing Cather published after she finished writing *The Professor's House*, her recent sense of achievement in that novel probably had something to do with the way she now thought of the proper role of the American novelist. And finally, there is her "letter" "On *The Professor's House*," where she describes the form of her book in ways that identify it as a work that deliberately takes its subject out of doors and therefore out of the drawing room:

> In my book I tried to make Professor St. Peter's house rather over-crowded and stuffy with new things; American proprieties, clothes, furs, petty ambitions, quivering jealousies—until one got rather stifled. Then I wanted to open the square window and let in the fresh air that blew off the Blue Mesa and the fine disregard of trivialities which was in Tom Outland's face and in his behaviour. (*On Writing* 31–32)

If these statements do not precisely demonstrate that Cather thought of herself as a western writer, they do show, and rather dramatically, how great a distance she had traveled from James's "The House of Fiction" or Wharton's *The House of Mirth* (1905). In fact, Wharton's *The Age of Innocence* (1920) was filled with just the sort of petty ambitions and quivering jealousies that Cather (and Edith Wharton, too, for that matter, though in a different way) found so stifling. The disenchantment with the modern age that Wharton expressed through Newland Archer corresponds to Cather's own:

> The difference [between the old generation and the new] is that these young people take it for granted that they're going to get whatever they want, and that we almost always took it for granted that we shouldn't. Only, I wonder—the thing one's so certain of in advance: can it ever make one's heart beat as wildly? (Wharton 306)

In opposition to Wharton's uncertainty and regret, Cather's Archbishop confronts time and change with the same sort of serenity she detected in Jewett, Hawthorne, and Twain. "Men travel faster now," says Eusabio, "but I do not know if they go to better things." "We must not try to know the future, Eusabio," is Latour's quiet reply. "It is better not" (*Death Comes for the Archbishop* 289). But Godfrey St. Peter, the historian, has not acquired this sense of calm acceptance; instead, at the end he is a man who will have to learn to live without "delight."

By the time Cather met him, Twain, the self-described "Father of History," had learned a similar lesson. His favorite daughter, Susy, and his wife, Olivia, were dead; the shame of his financial ruin and the exhausting efforts to recoup his fortunes had taken their toll on him; and his own several illnesses were, even on good days, wearying and annoying. These and other subtractions from his life contributed to Twain's pessimism in his last years. He was not without invention, however, and he spent much of his time not dwelling on last things but reimagining ancient beginnings, including the thoroughly humanized stories of Adam and Eve. Except for portions of Adam and Eve's "diaries," these writings remained unpublished at the time of his death, in part because he thought much of what he had to say was too scandalous for his public, but mostly because he could not find a satisfactory way to manage his material. He experimented with multiple narrators and recast previously written sections, but his imaginative ambitions, according to Howard Baetzhold and Joseph McCullough, were "simply too large to handle"; he wanted nothing less than to create a "documentary of a doomed civilization" (Twain, *Bible* 41). The three fragments that particularly interest Skaggs are parts of this larger design.

Whether one assents to Skaggs's proposal that at least a portion of those fragments constitutes a valentine from Twain to Cather or that Cather wished, in *The Professor's House*, to enter into a "dialog" with the now-dead Twain, the correspondences she amasses are impressive and her arguments intriguing. Her speculations bring us somewhat closer to the nature of Cather's imagination as it is enacted in precise and localizable ways and at the same time comment on the suggestiveness of their differences. It would be pointless to rehearse the argument of "Cather and the Father of History," since the reader has it ready at hand, but I do want to comment on certain features of the essay.

Skaggs notes that, taken separately, the parallels between the Twain fragments and *The Professor's House* may be nothing more than "small coincidences." Taken collectively, however, they begin to form a persuasive pattern. She further observes that much of what she has to say cannot be proved "beyond a shadow of a doubt," but she properly adds that it would be foolish and irresponsible to simply ignore or discount the correspondences and echoes she has detected. Since Skaggs invites us to picture a possible moment in the biography of Willa Cather, I would like to speculate on particular features of that moment, for they have implications for how we might better understand Cather and her novel *The Professor's House*.

I am especially interested in how Cather came by her invitation to Twain's birthday dinner at Delmonico's in 1905. James Woodress plausibly assumes that McClure must have given her an invitation. The guest list was an exclusive one, though; William Dean Howells thought the 172 people gathered at this "sky-scraping banquet" were the "strangest mixture of literary celebrity and social notoriety that I have ever seen" (qtd. in Crowley 86). Certainly, the occasion constituted a national celebration as well as a personal opportunity for an aspiring young writer. Perhaps Cather was, as Skaggs surmises, looking for a literary sponsor; we know she had something to peddle—the manuscript of a novel that McClure had recently rejected. But how canny was Cather in advancing her own professional aspirations? And how much did she need the kind of help and encouragement a figure like Twain might offer?

The Delmonico's dinner also offers an alternative explanation of how Cather might have become acquainted with unpublished Twain manuscripts. At the banquet, Cather was seated next to *Harper's* editor Frederick Duneka. Albert Bigelow Paine, Twain's authorized biographer, was also present at the affair. After Twain's death, Duneka and Paine cobbled out of several manuscripts what became known as *The Mysterious Stranger*. Of more immediate interest, however, is the fact that Paine was Twain's literary executor. He had authority over unpublished Twain manuscripts, and Duneka had access to Paine. Thanks to the seating arrangement at Delmonico's, Cather had access to Duneka. Might Duneka or Paine have allowed Cather to read in these materials? This line of inquiry would likely prove a dead end, I suspect, since Paine was not disposed to make Twain's unpublished manuscripts available to others.

Another, and perhaps more fruitful, lead might be pursuing Skaggs's invitation to imagine a closer and more confidential relationship between the relatively young aspiring writer and the "old lion." But how might Cather have separated herself from a host of admirers who came to visit and gain Twain's particular attention? And what sort of conversation would prompt Twain to talk about his unfinished work? One possible answer lies in the fact that Twain published *Christian Science, With Notes Containing Corrections to Date* in 1907, the same year S. S. McClure assigned Cather to do some fact-checking on Georgine Milmine's damning story of the life of Mary Baker Eddy. Twain, of course, would be eager to hear every unflattering detail Cather had to offer about the founder of Christian Science, and for her part, Cather would be obliged to read and perhaps hear about the factual "corrections" Twain made to his earlier essays on Eddy and Christian Science. In this imagined scenario, it is easy to envision Twain bringing out from a drawer his satirical piece of future history, "The Secret History of Eddypus, The World Empire," in which Christian Science has become the state religion and Twain himself appears as the "Bishop of New Jersey." Since this satire is in keeping with his other writings on "doomed civilization," it is certainly possible that he might have shared other writings with Cather, including the three fragments Skaggs isolates for our attention.

Skaggs's essay has provoked in me a decided curiosity about questions I never would have posed to myself. Was Cather a starstruck admirer of Mark Twain, or was she perhaps more calculating in her attention to him? Did she at some more or less datable time abandon her allegiances to James and Wharton and begin to think of herself, as she probably thought of Twain, as a western writer? Did Twain share manuscript fragments with her that disclose his dark thoughts on Western civilization, and did she recall them when she began writing *The Professor's House*, not long after her own thinking had taken a dark turn and she, in 1922, decided that the world "broke in two"? Are the echoes and parallels Skaggs discerns in Twain's and Cather's texts an homage to or an imagined collaboration with Twain himself? These and other questions have no certain answers. But I, at least, am grateful that Skaggs has brought these two great writers into active conversation with each other.

3. DEATH COMES FOR THE ARCHBISHOP

Fig. 1. Willa Cather, 1936. Carl Van Vechten, a lover of the Southwest, posed Cather under a *retablo* of Jesus entering Jerusalem on Palm Sunday. Courtesy of the Library of Congress.

Fig. 2. A nineteenth-century *bulto* of Santiago, a popular saint in New Mexico described by Jean Latour in *Death Comes for the Archbishop* as "wearing the costume of a Mexican *ranchero*, velvet trousers richly embroidered and wide at the ankle, velvet jacket and silk shirt, and a high-crowned, broad-brimmed Mexican sombrero" (28). Courtesy of the International Folk Art Foundation Collection in the Museum of International Folk Art, a unit of the Museum of New Mexico, Sante Fe. Photo by Blair Clark.

Fig. 3. A *bulto* of Our Lady of Sorrows (Nuestra Señora de los Dolores) by José Benito Ortega, ca. 1875–1907. Originally from Frank Applegate's collection. Courtesy of the Colorado Springs Fine Arts Center, Gift of Alice Bemis Taylor.

Fig. 4. Another example of a *bulto* of Our Lady of Sorrows. Courtesy of the Colorado Springs Fine Arts Center.

Fig. 5. This *bulto* of Our Lady of Solitude closely resembles the one Cather describes in Benito's home: "long and stiff and severe, very long from the neck to the waist, even longer from waist to feet" (28). From the school of José Benito Ortega, ca. 1875–1907. Courtesy of the Colorado Springs Fine Arts Center.

Fig. 6. Sacred Heart of Mary and Jesus (1850–1900), one of the lithographs that eroded the santos tradition. Courtesy of the Colorado Springs Fine Arts Center.

Fig. 7. This four-foot-tall *bulto* of Jesus Nazarene is more typical of those favored by the Penitential Brotherhood in the Taos area, ca. 1860–80. Courtesy of the Colorado Springs Fine Arts Center, gift of Alice Bemis Taylor.

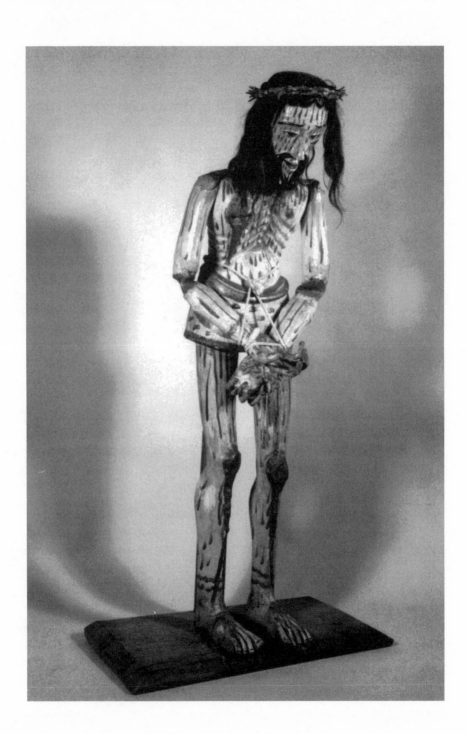

Fig. 8. Comparison of ornamental patterns of the cliff dwellers of Mesa Verde. From Gustaf Nordenskiöld, *The Cliff Dwellers of the Mesa Verde, Southwestern Colorado: Their Pottery and Implements* (1893; AMS, 1973).

Fig. 9. Cliff Palace before reconstruction. From Jesse Walter Fewkes, *Antiquities of the Mesa Verde National Park: Cliff Palace* (Bureau of American Ethnology, Bulletin 51, 1911).

Fig. 10. Cliff Palace after reconstruction. From Jesse Walter Fewkes, *Antiquities of the Mesa Verde National Park: Cliff Palace* (Bureau of American Ethnology, Bulletin 51, 1911).

Fig. 11. Tony Luhan, ca. 1920. Courtesy of the Beinecke Rare Book and Manuscript Library.

Mary Chinery

Willa Cather and the Santos Tradition
in *Death Comes for the Archbishop*

In early 1936 Willa Cather sat for one of two portraits by Carl Van Vechten, who had long been after her for his growing photograph collection of artists of the day. Cather, who disliked having her picture taken, had put off Van Vechten for as long as possible (Woodress 466), but he was persistent, calling on their mutual friends and publisher, the Knopfs, to intervene (Woodress 466). He wrote to Blanche Knopf, "I've told Miss Cather repeatedly she may come any time of day, even at dawn. . . . Please tell her she may set her own hour, but that I'd like to take her while America is still Royalist" (148). When Cather finally sat for the portrait in Van Vechten's home, she posed under a New Mexican *retablo*, an image that brings to mind their mutual love of the Southwest (fig. 1). The rare *retablo* "The Entry into Jerusalem" recalls both Jean Latour, the horse-mounted missionary in Cather's 1927 *Death Comes for the Archbishop*, and the New Mexican santos tradition, an overlooked inspiration for the novel.

Much of *Death Comes for the Archbishop* takes place in the northern New Mexican towns where the santos tradition flourished in the late nineteenth century, areas Willa Cather had traveled throughout on horseback and by car. These early sojourns, combined with her relationship with at least two well-known collectors of New Mexican folk art, Mary Austin and Mabel Dodge Luhan, make it very likely that Cather knew the santos tradition better than has been previously supposed and consciously incorporated it into her novel. Cather was also aware that the tradition was in danger of being sold off to people who would not care for it as well as those from the area. Cather was right: the santos tradition changed considerably between the time she first arrived in New Mexico in 1912 and the time *Death Comes for the Archbishop* was published some fifteen years later.

Cather's knowledge of the santos complements her already well-known passion for the fine arts, which both James Woodress and John J. Murphy have addressed. In her letter to *Commonweal* on the novel, Cather points to Holbein's *Dance of Death* and Puvis de Chavannes's *St. Geneviève at Prayer* as particular inspirations. Cather had written to *Commonweal* to answer questions about the novel and about the rumor that she was Roman Catholic, but the letter also reveals her fascination with the local religious art of the Southwest. She describes the santos as "the countless fanciful figures of the saints, no two of them alike, [which] seemed a direct expression of some very real and lively human feeling. They were all fresh, individual, first-hand" (*On Writing* 5–6). Cather expounds at more length on local church art than on European art in that letter. Few secondary sources, however, have acknowledged in detail Cather's debt to local religious art in the composition of *Death Comes for the Archbishop*. One exception is Kevin Synott, who, in his essay on the visual and pictorial elements of the novel, describes the santos as "the Mexican icons—the rough, hand-carved wooden figures of the saints, brightly painted and dressed—[which] become simplified versions of their more sophisticated counterparts" in the European saints (13). Evelyn Haller has done the most thorough examination to date, writing about Hispanic folk traditions as one of the four complementary worldviews that structure Cather's novel: Francocentric, medieval iconographic, Mexican, and Native American. As Haller writes, "Cather's own delight in santos emphasizes her recognition of experimental modern as well as folk forms" of art (18).

Santos come in two forms: *retablos*, flat pictures painted on cottonwood, and *bultos*, three-dimensional carved figures of varying sizes. Emerging from Spanish traditions that traveled to the New World, the santos were adopted by the Franciscans in their early missionary days to provide Christian devotional art in the churches (Frank 4). After the 1680 Pueblo Revolt removed the priests and Spanish from the area, Don Diego de Vargas returned with families in 1692 to reestablish the Spanish presence in New Mexico. Larry Frank explains that the santos first developed a Mexican flavor more in tune with European traditions, including lifelike statues, bodies in proper proportion, and some ornate dress. Then, as Hispanic settlements moved northward, a distinctive New Mexican style developed, one that used elongated bodies—rather than realistic bodies—either simply dressed in cloth or painted over the wood. Frank writes that as the tradition developed,

Their santos no longer reflected a conscious emulation of Old World styles, but were, instead, original interpretations of religious iconography, made within the context of the social, cultural, and spiritual influences of New Mexico; they and their followers established a decidedly New Mexican style of santo that is unique to the Southwest. (13–14)

These santos thrived in what has been called a classic period, from about 1790 until 1860, though that style continued until around 1907, when José Benito Ortega and Juan de Dios Herrera—among the last known *santeros* of the period—gave it up (Frank 29, 32). A *santero* ("saint-maker") looked upon his art as a sacred calling and frequently traveled to take orders for his carvings (Frank 26). *Santeros* worked within existing subjects and with common images: the trinity, Christ crucified, Mary, and local saints. However, each *santero* developed his own interpretation of facial features or expressions by which he is identified today (Steele 11). Thirty thousand to forty thousand santos were created during this era in which each home owned a few for family devotion (Frank 14).

Modern *santeros* continue until this day, but the classic style faded with the importation of chromolithographs and premade factory forms from Mexico and Europe (Wroth xvi) that Latour describes in *Death Comes for the Archbishop* as "the factory-made plaster images in his mission churches in Ohio" (28). Catholic and Protestant churches alike preferred these lithographs over the santos, and they are frequently seen in later-era church altar screens (Frank 32–33). As early as 1776, an order from the archdiocese of Durango, followed by additional orders over the years, banished santos from the churches (Boyd 23). William Wroth writes that such "widely recognized symbols of piety were seen by the newcomers as exotic relics of an antiquated [Penitential] cult" (xvi). Hence it was left to the people to preserve the santos either by ignoring the orders of church authorities or by collecting them for their homes.

Though the santos emerged from old Mexico and New Mexico, there was a particular hold on the tradition in the rugged northern part of New Mexico and in southern Colorado. Towns noted for their *santeros* include Abiquiú, Cordova, Mora, Taos, and Arroyo Hondo, areas Cather traveled through or that figure into *Death Comes for the Archbishop*.

Cather's journeys to the Southwest began in 1912, when she traveled there to see her brother Douglass, then living in Arizona. Subsequent trips in 1914 took her to Wyoming, Arizona, and New Mexico. In 1915 she returned to New Mexico, this time visiting Mesa Verde, Colorado, and Taos, New Mexico. Taos was not yet an art colony, and to get around Cather rode on horseback or hired a team (Woodress 265). When she visited Santa Fe and Taos again in 1916, she traveled in the areas where the santos remained: "There were in addition lovely little villages lying about everywhere, and she could visit five or six of them every morning on her daily horseback ride" (Woodress 281). However, after discovering Jaffrey, New Hampshire, she did not return to the area until 1925.

By the late teens, artists and writers drawn to the southwestern landscape and climate created art colonies, particularly in the Santa Fe and Taos areas where Cather had already traveled extensively. Among those she knew in Santa Fe were Witter Bynner, with whom both Cather and Edith Lewis had worked at *McClure's*. Mary Austin, who had also been visiting the area since the late teens, built a home in Santa Fe in 1924. Austin and Cather had a warm correspondence for ten years, which began after Austin had written an article on Cather in the late teens. According to T. M. Pearce, when Austin moved to New York, Cather wrote to say she hoped they would be neighbors and later invited her to a few of her Friday afternoon teas (203). "Cather expressed both curiosity and envy" when Austin moved to Santa Fe (Pearce 203), where she collected folk art and stories of the area, culminating in her founding of the Spanish Colonial Arts Society with sculptor Frank Applegate.

Considering the two writers' friendship, it seems likely that they had read each other's work. Janis P. Stout convincingly argues that Cather knew Austin's *A Woman of Genius* (1912) as she wrote *The Song of the Lark* (1915) (44). It therefore does not seem surprising, though there is no positive proof, that Cather read Austin's *The Land of Journeys' Ending* (1924), a poetic history of New Mexico and its customs, in preparation for writing *Death Comes for the Archbishop*. In particular, she might have been interested in a chapter titled "The Saints in Mexico" in which Austin describes the role of the saints, especially the Virgin Mary, in the daily lives of people and details the fiestas and saints' days. A passage Cather would have found especially useful describes Austin's understanding of miracle in the context of New Mexican spiritual culture:

> For I have written thus far in vain if you do not begin to understand that New Mexico is still a place in which the miraculous may happen. All myth, all miracle, is in the beginning a notice of a Borning in the deep self; new ideas, new concepts of spiritual reality making their way to expression in whatever stuff is current in the mind of the locality.(337)

Latour expresses to Vaillant his idea of miracle far more simply when he says, regarding the Virgin of Guadalupe,

The Miracles of the Church seem to me to rest not so much upon faces or voices or healing power coming suddenly near to us from afar off, but upon our perceptions being made finer, so that for a moment our eyes can see and our ears can hear what is there about us always. (50)

The end of the friendship between Cather and Austin is well known: during the final months of the composition of *Death Comes for the Archbishop*, Cather stayed at the La Fonda Hotel in Santa Fe and wrote at Austin's house in the morning while her hostess was having surgery. Their correspondence came to an abrupt end, however, with Austin's publication of her autobiography *Earth Horizon* (1932). There she excoriated Cather's novel, calling her fictionalized hero and his cathedral a "calamity to the local culture" (Austin, *Earth Horizon* 359). Although Cather thereafter denied writing anything at all at Austin's home, they nonetheless exchanged four letters before Austin's death in 1934 (Pearce 205).

Cather also knew Mabel Dodge Luhan, a socialite and promoter of the arts who amassed a collection of santos. Luhan first visited the West with her husband, artist Maurice Sterne, but stayed after marrying Tony Luhan, a Taos Indian. As the doyenne of the avant-garde salon in Cather's Greenwich Village, she may have known Cather in the early teens. Woodress writes that Cather "may have attended Mabel Dodge's famous salon on occasion, as everyone in Greenwich Village seems to have gone there, but her friendship with Dodge came after she married Tony Luhan and was living in New Mexico" (236). In a phrase that echoes Cather, Luhan writes in *Edge of the Taos Desert* (1937) that when she moved to the Southwest, "my life broke in two right then, and I entered into the second half, a new world that replaced all the ways I had known with others" (6). She built a large home with multiple compounds near the pueblo in Taos for the purpose of nurturing the many artists she had met over the years. After a few requests, Cather finally agreed to stay with Luhan in the private guest house D. H. Lawrence and his wife, Frieda, had occupied. Here Cather traveled by car with Tony Luhan to places where the santos were quite well established (Woodress 363).

As Luhan explains in her autobiography, a modernist mania for santos occurred almost as soon as artists moved to the Southwest in the late teens and twenties. Soon after her arrival with Sterne, she started collecting Mexican folk art. Artist Andrew Dasburg accompanied Luhan and Sterne on jaunts to purchase blankets and santos, paying about a dollar for each of the wooden figures. She writes that Dasburg

> hunted the old Santos painted on hand-hewn boards that we had discovered soon after we came to Taos. No one had ever noticed them except to laugh, but here was an authentic primitive art, quite unexploited. We were, I do believe, the first people who ever bought them from the Mexicans. (125–26)

They were so common in the area that "They were hanging in every Mexican house and chapel when we came here," and after a short time the Mexicans would come to the door to sell them (126). Dasburg and art collector Dr. Albert Barnes wanted them so badly that Dasburg "bullied" the Mexicans to give up the ones they did not want to sell (126); Barnes, for his part, ran through Luhan's house "like a madman" and begged to have the two santos in her cupboards, which she flatly refused, resulting in the eventual erosion of their friendship (127–28). "They belong here with my primitives," Luhan reports he wrote her (128). Luhan purchased her own and bought the ones Dasburg "did not care for, so those and the ones I found for myself made a real collection before long. I had them in our house for years" (127). In 1919 she sent her collection east to be shown in Tarrytown, New York, along with children's art from the Santa Fe Indian School. Art dealer Stephen Bourgeois saw the show and brought it to his gallery in Manhattan (Rudnick, *Mabel* 171). As a result, what had once been thought of as cheap, primitive religious artifacts became—with the development of art colonies in the Southwest—collectors' items, and subsequently a market for them developed. Eventually, Luhan donated her collection to the Harwood Foundation Museum.

In the *Commonweal* letter, Cather comments directly on the commodification of the folk art of New Mexico:

> May I say here that within the last few years some of the newer priests down in that country have been taking away from those old churches their homely images and decorations, which have a definite artistic and historic value, and replacing them by conventional, factory-made church furnishings from New York? It is a great pity. All Catholics will be sorry about it, I think, when it is too late, when all those old paintings and images and carved doors that have so much feeling and individuality are gone—sold to some collector in New York or Chicago, where they mean nothing. (*On Writing* 6)

She knew that as the market for the santos increased, they would be moved from their original context in a sacred space to private collections where the people who created them would no longer see them. No doubt she was also aware of the frenzy for collecting them.

In a sense, the *retablo* "Jesus' Entry into Jerusalem," with which I began the investigation of the santos, also begins our understanding of Latour in *Death Comes for the Archbishop*. The *retablo* alludes to Jesus' triumphant entry into Jerusalem before the Last Supper, his personal crises of faith in the garden of Gethsemane, and his crucifixion. The *retablo's* image is reminiscent of our introduction to Latour, who, traveling by horse, also experiences his own crucifixion of doubt, discombobulation, and thirst in "The Cruciform Tree." As he journeys, he struggles for images to express his confusion. The hills, he corrects himself, were "more the shape of Mexican ovens than haycocks— yes, exactly the shape of Mexican ovens, red as brick-dust" (17). Haycocks would be familiar to Latour from his home in France. Jean-François Millet, the French artist whom Cather loved, was known for depictions of rural life in paintings such as *Haystacks* and *The Gleaners*. However, Latour has lost his cultural bearings in a landscape so visually foreign to him that he searches for a way to explain his dislocation.

After being confused in "some geometrical nightmare" (17) and fearing for his life, Latour finds himself before a cruciform tree, where he prays. Rounding the hill, he is welcomed by what appears to be a mirage of river, green grass, and animals, whereupon he is greeted by a woman who explains that he has found an oasis called *Agua Secreta*, or Hidden Water (25). Latour is taken to the woman's father, Benito, a widower. Significantly, our first introduction to the Mexicans in the novel is this scene of hospitality. After a simple, nourishing supper, we are introduced to the santos in their proper context, an ordinary home. It is here that Latour first notices Benito's santos, in this case the three-dimensional carvings called *bultos* (fig. 2):

> After supper Father Latour took up a candle and began to examine the holy images on the shelf over the fireplace. The wooden figures of the saints, found in even the poorest Mexican houses, always interested him. He had never yet seen two alike. These over Benito's fireplace had come in the ox-carts from Chihuahua nearly sixty years ago. They had been carved by some devout soul, and brightly painted, though the colours had softened with time, and they were dressed in cloth, like dolls. (27–28)

Latour has seen and admired santos before, noting their originality, coloring, and age. They are also a link to his home culture, for they were more "like the homely stone carvings on the front of old parish churches in Auvergne"

(28). According to Thomas Steele, santos, unlike European religious art, were meant as not only devotional objects but as daily, physical links between heaven and earth (Steele 85). The same santo was suitable for both church and home. As we see, the day after Latour's arrival, "the sorrowful wooden Virgin" was taken down from her mantle to become the focal point of the altar, decorated simply with flowers and candles (30).

Latour mentions three santos in particular: St. Joseph, Mary, and Santiago, each with personal resonance in the family and in the novel. Joseph is the patron saint of Benito's daughter Josepha and Latour's friend Joseph Vaillant, who figures prominently in the novel. Santiago is the namesake of Benito's younger grandson, who explains to Latour the saint's purpose in Mexican religious culture. Mary, the most popular image in Mexican homes, is a named and unnamed presence throughout the novel.

Cather describes Mary quite precisely: "dressed in black, with a white apron, and a black reboso over her head, like a Mexican woman of the poor" (28). She, like many of the santos, is a painted wooden frame dressed in cloth. Mary figures were quite common and came in many forms, including Our Lady of Solitude, Our Lady of Mount Carmel, Our Lady of the Rosary, and Our Lady of Light, each often with a devotional society in her honor in Santa Fe (Cash 221). Known by particular colors, dress, and pose, each one would be recognized by the faithful. Latour says of the Mary figure, "The wooden Virgin was a sorrowing mother indeed,—long and stiff and severe, very long from the neck to the waist, even longer from waist to feet" (28). Clearly stylized and out of proportion, this New Mexican *bulto* could be one of two popular images of Mary: Our Lady of Sorrows or Our Lady of Solitude (figs. 3, 4, and 5). Our Lady of Solitude is so called because she stood at the foot of the cross after Jesus was abandoned by his apostles. Also a sorrowing woman, she is generally painted in black, frequently with hands outstretched (Frank 307).

Another possible source for this image is Our Lady of Sorrows, whose name in Spanish is *Nuestra Señora de los Doloros*. Cather uses this Spanish appellation later in the novel when Latour refers to the "dolorous Virgins and the very human figures of the saints" (142). Next to Guadalupe, the best-known Mexican incarnation of Mary, "Our Lady of Sorrows is the most popular manifestation of the Virgin" (Frank 157). Often painted in red or blue, she is depicted with hands folded at her heart, sometimes with a sword or crown of thorns, which underscores the piercing of her suffering. Images of Mary are probably the most common of the santos.

Later in the novel, another image of Mary becomes important. Cather includes Our Lady of the Rosary, also known as La Conquistadora, who had a chapel in her honor under the jurisdiction of the Archbishop (Cash 222). She was thirty-three inches tall and created in approximately 1626, according to the initial survey of santos by Fray Dominguez in 1776 (Cash 214). Cather describes her as "a little wooden figure, about three feet high, very stately in bearing, with a beautiful though rather severe Spanish face" and as "very old and very dear to the people" (254). The confraternity of Our Lady of the Rosary, which dates to 1625 in Santa Fe, was apparently the one de Vargas carried into battle, promising a yearly procession in her honor if he won (Murphy 488). Whereas the historical Archbishop Lamy had little interest in the confraternity, Cather's Latour allows the people their traditions in her honor. Indeed, Latour "had delighted her wardrobe keepers when he told them he did not believe the Queen of England or the Empress of France had so many costumes" (254). Cather likens the people's love of this image to their desire to build cathedrals for her, each an impulse of the human heart to reach outward and upward.

Benito owns "a fierce little equestrian figure" identified by Latour as Santiago (28), "a saint wearing the costume of a Mexican *ranchero*, velvet trousers richly embroidered and wide at the ankle, velvet jacket and silk shirt, and a high-crowned, broad-brimmed Mexican sombrero" (28). According to Steele, Santiago, a Mexican version of the popular European St. James, appeared on a horse in a Spanish battle against the Moors (71–72). St. Jacques, as he is known in France, has particular interest for Latour on his journey, for he was known as the patron saint of those on pilgrimage and, as Latour explains, is also the protector of missionaries. In France, Santiago is depicted on foot with a walking stick. Benito's grandson Santiago explains that in Mexico he is the patron saint of horses, adding, "He blesses the mares and makes them fruitful" or "the foals do not come right" (29). Santiago also became the protector of the Spanish against Native Americans (Steele 72). Thus his "fierce" appearance and dress as a well-off ranchero in local clothing suggest the success of Spanish colonialism.

Though Latour likes the santos, he is ambivalent about the colorful fiestas and festivals of the faithful, for "[i]n his own country all this would have been highly distasteful" to him (142). Part of those spectacles were the Penitential Brotherhood's Holy Week ceremonies, to which Cather alludes indirectly in her *Commonweal* letter when she writes, "In lonely, sombre villages in the mountains the church decorations were sombre, the martyrdoms bloodier, the grief of the Virgin more agonized, the figure of Death more terrifying" (5). The villages Cather references were those around Taos that she toured on horseback during her first trip to the Southwest, then later by car with Tony Luhan.

The Penitential Brotherhood, which served as a fraternal organization and was held in great esteem among the people, also helped preserve the santos tradition. In the years priests were difficult to come by, the group held prayer services to aid the faithful. The group's relationship with the official Roman Catholic Church, however, had always been tenuous, particularly before and after Archbishop Lamy's tenure. The brotherhood was viewed as "out-of-date, unprogressive, and even socially harmful" (Wroth xvi). Marta Weigle writes that Lamy approved rules for the organization in 1853 but that by 1879 he was frustrated by their rejection of some of those rules (53, 57). Overall, however, "[h]is condemnation of the Penitentes was never vehement, and he seems to have left the more direct attacks to his successor" (57). Their Holy Week practices, which included flagellation and the rumored crucifixion of one member, became well known in the 1920s. In *Death Comes for the Archbishop*, Trinidad Lucero exemplifies these practices. As Kit Carson's wife tells Latour,

> He was tied upon a cross with ropes, to hang there all night; they do that sometimes at Abiquiu, it is a very old-fashioned place. But he is so heavy that after he had hung there a few hours, the cross fell over with him, and he was very much humiliated. (154)

Trinidad then had himself whipped, but he fainted, so the Penitentes did not want him to return. Señora Carson advised Latour to let things with the Penitentes remain as they were: "It would only set the people against you. The old people have need of their old customs; and the young ones will go with the times" (154–55).

The santos tradition waned after the Roman Catholic Church officially discouraged the use of the santos and because of the advent of lithography (fig. 6). The Penitentes collected all the santos they could, and commissioned particular figures for their Holy Week ceremonies, which kept later *santeros*, such as José Benito Ortega, busy into the early years of the twentieth century. In *Death Comes for the Archbishop* Cather calls them "agonized Christs" (142). Frequently much larger than the typical santos, these Jesus figures bear the bloody marks of the scourgings that the Penitentes themselves incurred during Easter processions (fig. 7).

Cather loved the santos and the other Hispanic folk arts she found in her travels throughout the Southwest, and she lovingly integrated them into *Death Comes for the Archbishop*. Far from being hostile to Mexican culture over the French American influence in Mexico, Cather unobtrusively weaves folk art into her novel of fine art, showing a clear understanding of the history and context of the santos. As she wrote in *Commonweal*, "There are other ways of telling what one feels, and the people who built and decorated those many, many little churches found their way and left their message" (*On Writing* 6).

Christopher Schedler

Writing Culture

Willa Cather's Southwest

> *The first thing an artist does when he begins a new work is to lay down the barriers and limitations; he decides upon a certain composition, a certain key, a certain relation of creatures or objects to each other . . . , and unless he is more interested in his own little story and his foolish little people than in the Preservation of the Indian or Sex or Tuberculosis, then he ought to be working in a laboratory or a bureau.–Willa Cather, "Light on Adobe Walls"*

In this essay, I trace the development of Willa Cather's aesthetic, in particular her emphasis on the formal "relation of creatures or objects to each other," as manifested in the interaction of cultures depicted in her southwestern fiction. Furthermore, I argue that her interaction with the cultures of the Southwest had a direct influence on both her understanding of culture and her developing aesthetic practices. By drawing on developments in anthropology and modes of ethnography, I examine Cather's writing of culture as it engages with theories of cultural evolutionism, cultural relativism, and cultural borderlands. On the aesthetic level, developments in her understanding of culture correspond to her formal experiments with the "relation of creatures or objects to each other," methods I characterize as comparison, juxtaposition, and dialogism. These ethnographic and aesthetic classifications help us map the Southwest as represented by Cather: through the cultural evolutionism and comparative method of *The Song of the Lark* (1915), the cultural relativism and juxtaposition of *The Professor's House* (1925), and the cultural borderlands and dialogism of *Death Comes for the Archbishop* (1927).

Cather's initial understanding of culture, as represented in *The Song of the Lark*, follows a nineteenth-century romantic theory of cultural evolutionism. In his historiography of anthropological approaches toward culture, George W. Stocking Jr. suggests that cultural evolutionism was "methodologically dependent on the idea of progress in all realms of human activity," relying on a "comparative method" that "attempted to arrange the coexisting manifestations of human culture in temporal sequences of progressive development which were ordered in a singular cultural hierarchy at whose peak stood western European civilization" (228). In the late nineteenth and early twentieth centuries there was little

> distinction between race, language, and culture, in a period when almost any human group—whether linguistic, religious, or national—might be called a "race." . . . Races were often thought of as supraindividual entities which had a common "genius" or "soul," or whose existence on earth followed the individual human life cycle of birth, growth, maturity, and perhaps even death. (65)

Cultural evolutionism thus distinguished between distinct human groups (or "races"), each following its own cycle of development, which could be placed within a hierarchy of evolutionary stages along a historical continuum from savagery to civilization.

Cather's *The Song of the Lark* tells the story of Thea Kronborg's development from a precocious child growing up in the small town of Moonstone, Colorado, to the Wagnerian opera star performing in every European and American metropolis. In this autobiographical novel, Thea undergoes an artistic rebirth in the Southwest similar to the one Cather experienced during her first trip there in 1912 (*On Writing* 92). In particular, Cather's explorations of the cliff dwellings of Walnut Canyon, Arizona, are replayed in Thea's experiences in the cliff-dweller ruins of Panther Canyon. Cather's approach to this indigenous culture of the Southwest exhibits the cultural evolutionism and comparative method found in the work of amateur European archaeologist Gustaf Nordenskiöld, whose pioneering study *The Cliff Dwellers of the Mesa Verde* Cather most likely read before her visit to Mesa Verde in the summer of 1915, the same year *The Song of the Lark* was completed and published. (David Harrell suggests that Cather read Nordenskiöld's book before she visited Mesa Verde in 1915 since the book was probably unavailable at the park at that time and could most likely only be found in a metropolitan library [14].) Nordenskiöld's book is an important source for *The Professor's House*, which includes the fictional story of Tom Outland's discovery of the Cliff Palace, the most famous cliff-dweller ruin in Mesa Verde. However, the connections between Nordenskiöld's book and Cather's earlier novel *The Song of the Lark* have yet to be explored.

In *The Song of the Lark*, Henry Biltmer, an old German who runs the ranch at Panther Canyon for Fred Ottenburg's father, views the cliff dwellers in terms similar to those employed by Nordenskiöld in his study of the cliff dwellers of Mesa Verde. Biltmer explains to Thea "that the Ancient People had developed masonry and pottery far beyond any other crafts" (272). Likewise, Nordenskiöld suggests that

> the former inhabitants of the cliff-dwellings were *an agricultural people on the level of the Stone Age*, who had attained a very high rank in the art of making and ornamenting pottery and in the construction of stone buildings, but who at the same time stood comparatively low in other respects. (20, italics in original)

Here Nordenskiöld comparatively ranks cultural practices within a hierarchy of "progress" toward western European notions of a "civilized" culture, including aesthetic notions of ornamental beauty: "The ornamentation of the earthenware also betokens a certain sense of beauty, a quality which we have no opportunity of observing in other productions of the cliff-people's industry" (76–77; fig. 8). The work of this late-nineteenth-century archaeologist clearly exhibits the theory and comparative method of cultural evolutionism.

In *The Song of the Lark*, Biltmer's comparison between the "stupid women" who "carried water for most of their lives" and the "cleverer ones" who "made the vessels to hold it" couples Nordenskiöld's ethnographic hierarchy and Cather's apotheosis of the artist (272). Using the comparative approach of cultural evolutionism, Cather represents cliff-dweller culture as an origin point for the general "progress" of civilization and the development of an artistic sensibility in particular, beginning with the "Ancient People" and culminating with the European opera star:

> All these things made one feel that one ought to do one's best, and help fulfill some desire of the dust that slept there. . . . In their own way, those people had felt the beginnings of what was to come. These potsherds were like fetters that bound one to a long chain of human endeavor. (275)

Biltmer's ethnographic reading of the women's pottery as "their most direct appeal to water, the envelope and sheath of the precious element itself" thus becomes the basis for Thea's artistic epiphany at the bottom of Panther Canyon: "The stream and the broken pottery: what was any art but an effort to make a sheath, a mould in which to imprison for a moment the shining, elusive element which is life itself" (273).

The same ideology of "progress" and comparative method, which enable the sequential arrangement of peoples in a singular hierarchy of cultural evolution, function on an aesthetic level to structure Cather's novel. In comparison to the experimental narrative techniques Cather employed in works like *The Professor's House* and *Death Comes for the Archbishop*, *The Song of the Lark* appears highly conventional: it is based on a linear, sequential, and hierarchical model that follows a chronological timeline, proceeds by cause and effect, and reaches an apex with a climax event deemed to be the most significant. Along these lines, events and characters are narratively arranged solely in relation to Thea's artistic development. The other characters are merely the "halfway people" Ray Kennedy identifies, those "who help the winners win, and the failers fail" (126). The chapter titles help us trace Thea's development in relation to these "halfway people": the "Friends of Childhood" and "The Ancient People" help her win, while the "Stupid Faces" attempt to make her fail. Similarly, narrative events such as Ray's death (which provides Thea with the money to go to Chicago) and Fred Ottenburg's appearance (which provides her with a means of escape from Chicago) inexorably lead to the climactic moment of Thea's artistic epiphany in Panther Canyon. This accounts for the subsequent "descending curve," which Cather identified as the "chief fault" of her novel in the preface to the 1932 edition (O'Brien, introduction vii).

In *The Professor's House*, Cather imaginatively returned to the Southwest and the cliff dwellers, but this time with a new understanding of cultures and the "relation of creatures or objects to each other." This new understanding most likely began to develop after Cather had completed *The Song of the Lark* and visited Mesa Verde in 1915. Cather and her companion Edith Lewis spent a week at the ruins and a full day exploring the famous Cliff Palace. They also found themselves lost in Soda Canyon with an inexperienced guide and had to wait on a rock for four or five hours while their guide searched for a nearby archaeologist's camp. Fortunately, men from the camp appeared and led them back to the diggings of Dr. Jesse Walter Fewkes (Woodress 263–64). Fewkes was a Smithsonian archaeologist who worked in Mesa Verde from 1908 to 1926 and wrote more than thirty papers on his findings. (See Watson Smith's introduction to Nordenskiöld's work, xii.) While visiting Mesa Verde, Cather most likely saw a park brochure that can be traced to Fewkes's hand and may have read his work in other venues after meeting him. (In *From Mesa Verde*,

Harrell does a fine job of tracing connections between Cather's novel and Fewkes's work, 20–24.) Stocking identifies Fewkes as a supporter of Franz Boas, whose notion of cultural relativism was the basis of modern cultural anthropology (290).

Stocking notes that Boas's critique of the theory and method of cultural evolutionism revealed the implausibility of a singular, evolutionary system of culture common to all humankind and replaced it with the modern anthropological model of a multiplicity of converging and diverging cultures produced in relation to distinct historical and environmental processes (212). Thus, unlike Nordenskiöld's placement of the cliff dwellers within a singular hierarchy of culture "progress" from Stone Age to "civilized" man, Fewkes investigates cliff-dweller culture as "one type of prehistoric American culture" (11). Boas's method was to shift attention away from those features common to various human groupings and focus instead on the differences that distinguished individual groups. Boas also replaced the comparative method of evolutionism with the modern anthropological method of participatory observation, which depended upon the fieldworker's acceptance of cultural relativism: the withholding of judgment based upon personal opinions and emotions or external standards. As Stocking suggests,

> Once the "one grand scheme" of evolutionism was rejected, the multiplicity of *cultures* which took the place of the cultural *stages* of savagery, barbarism, and civilization were no more easily brought within one standard of evaluation than they were within one system of explanation.
> (229, italics in original)

Cultural anthropologists analyzed individual ethnological specimens not within a singular hierarchy of culture but rather within the historical and cultural context of the specific group that produced them: "the individualities Boas was concerned with were not so much those of individual specimens as of each tribal culture as a subjectively perceived whole" (Stocking 156). Cultural relativism thus held in tension an objective method of collecting individual cultural specimens, which required withholding personal judgment, and a subjective method of analysis, by which the cultural interpreter constructed a cultural unity within which those individual specimens could be understood (figs. 9 and 10).

Boas's concern with the relationship between objective knowledge of the external world and subjective knowledge of others, as well as with the epistemological problem of our knowledge, mirrors one of the major concerns of *The Professor's House*. The central section of Cather's novel, "Tom

Outland's Story," is essentially an ethnographic text, concerned primarily with interpreting and writing the culture uncovered in the cliff-dweller ruins. However, this text also becomes the central piece of an epistemological puzzle, a series of mediations that continually displaces the story's objects of knowledge: cliff-dweller culture for Tom Outland and Tom Outland for the novel's protagonist, Professor St. Peter. The written text of "Tom Outland's Story" is presented as St. Peter's reminiscence of Tom's oral retelling of his "discovery" and archaeological exploration of the Cliff City of Blue Mesa. These subjective reminiscences are themselves predicated upon an absent written text, Tom's "diary," the objective record of each "specimen" uncovered in his archaeological excavations: "where and in what condition we had found it, and what we thought it had been used for" (189). Drawing on the methods of Boasian cultural anthropology, we might say this objective record of collected specimens becomes the basis for Tom's subjective interpretation of cliff-dweller culture. Likewise, the "diary," in which "there was almost nothing about Tom himself," requires an introduction by St. Peter to the subject of Tom Outland before it can be published (150). Just as the "lost" culture of the cliff dwellers becomes meaningful only through the subjective musings of the cultural interpreter—Tom Outland—the meaning of Tom Outland resides not in the objective record of the diary but in the subjective interpretation of St. Peter.

Tom's approach to cliff-dweller culture aligns him with the cultural relativism of Boasian anthropology. Tom is presented as the model cultural anthropologist, engaging in what would come to be known as "salvage" anthropology, an effort to collect the cultural artifacts of "vanishing" American Indian tribes. Tom approaches cliff-dweller culture with the desire to "understand it, . . . appreciate it and dig out all its secrets" (202). Unlike the museums, which appear only interested in tracing the origins of European civilization by displaying "something that came from Crete or Egypt," Tom is interested in "our things," that is, the cultural artifacts of America (102). As a cultural relativist, Tom is concerned with what the cliff-dweller artifacts reveal about the historical and cultural processes that shaped America rather than with what they reveal about the "progress" of civilization, understood in western European terms. For example, he defends "Indian housewifery" and prefers turquoises the way Indians like them, in their original state, "before the jewellers have tampered with them and made them look green" (102).

Tom also exhibits a Boasian preference for viewing each tribal culture as a subjectively perceived whole rather than as an objective collection of individual specimens. Tom's epiphany about the meaning of the Blue Mesa occurs the night he returns after the disappearance of his friend Roddy Blake, who has sold their Indian artifacts to a German collector: "This was the first time I ever saw it as a whole. It all came together in my understanding, as a series of experiments do when you begin to see where they are leading" (226). For Tom, this subjective perception of the whole in a sense eliminates the need for the lost parts (the artifacts) and for the objective record of those parts in his diary, which he leaves on the mesa before returning years later with Professor St. Peter to recover it: "I didn't feel the need of that record. It would have been going backward. I didn't want to go back and unravel things step by step. Perhaps I was afraid that I would lose the whole in the parts" (228). This Boasian concern for the proper relation between objective and subjective knowledge of other cultures becomes, in Cather's novel, the basis for her meditation on the epistemological problem of how one knows others and ultimately one's self.

The dissolution of Tom's friendship with Roddy occurs over their different interpretations of the cliff-dweller artifacts, the different meanings and values they assign to these cultural objects. Tom's disinterested and objective collection of the artifacts for scientific purposes, which he dutifully records in his diary, seems violated by Roddy's view of the Indian relics as commodities to be sold for personal gain, even if it is Tom who gains the money to go to college. However, their argument and Tom's subsequent epiphany reveal that Tom's apparent objectivity masks his own motivations. For the orphaned Tom—whose parents died while he was a baby in transit across the prairie—without a family, home, or even knowledge of his own age, the mesa becomes his "home" (217), the artifacts become his inheritance, and the cliff dwellers become his family (219). He calls his vision of the "whole" mesa "possession" and regards his feelings for the place as "filial piety" (227). Cather clearly shows how the apparent objectivity of cultural relativism remains predicated upon subjective relations to the object of knowledge, here the artifacts of cliff-dweller culture.

Cather further suggests that the objective truth of this other culture remains permanently beyond the grasp of the subjective meanings and values imposed upon it by cultural interpreters. In this regard, it seems quite appropriate that the most highly personified artifact of the cliff-dweller culture, the mummy christened Mother Eve, should be frozen in a silent scream; the cultural "other" as object of knowledge is here unable to reply to the subjective interpretations assigned to it (192). Likewise, that she "refused to leave" the mesa, falling to the bottom of the canyon along with the mule hired by the German collector to transport her out, suggests the violations of Native American cultural property rights when cultural "others" and their artifacts are viewed as objects of knowledge and removed by "salvage" anthropologists (221). (The scene brings to mind, for example, Leslie Marmon Silko's critique of white ethnologists such as Boas who collected Native American cultural materials as if they were public property.) If Cather exposes in "Tom Outland's Story" the seemingly unbridgeable gap within cultural relativism between subjective interpretations and the unknowable objective reality of the cultural "other," the rest of the novel extends this epistemological problem by exploring Professor St. Peter's attempt to interpret the meaning of Tom Outland and his attempts to understand his own divided self.

Like the "vanished" cliff dwellers, Tom, killed in World War I, is an absent presence at the center of Cather's novel, surviving only as a memory in the minds of the other characters. Just as Tom and others attempt to interpret the meaning and value of cliff-dweller culture, so do St. Peter and the rest of his family attempt to define Tom. To St. Peter, Tom represents youthful desire, the central element in creation and achievement (19). By dying young, Tom appears to have escaped the "trap of worldly success" in which the Professor feels caught, doomed to repeat the same "meaningless conventional gestures" without ever again creating something new like his great history of the *Spanish Adventurers in North America* (237). To the Professor, attempting to reconcile himself to the lost past of his youth and the prospect of a meaningless future, "Tom Outland's Story" is "nothing very incriminating, nothing very remarkable; a story of youthful defeat" (155). As we have seen, however, Tom is incriminated in a form of appropriation of cliff-dweller culture (what he calls "possession") based on his personal desire for home, inheritance, and family. What distinguishes Tom from Roddy, in Tom's and, apparently, the Professor's mind, is that Tom's appropriation is in the service of ideals, whereas Roddy's is in service of monetary gain. As St. Peter imagines Tom, "He idealized the people he loved and paid his devoir to the ideal rather than to the individual" (151), and he "had never handled things that were not the symbols of ideas" (236). If Tom appears to the Professor to base his relations with others on an ideal "dream of self-sacrificing friendship and disinterested love," we have seen that Tom's relation to cliff-dweller culture as an object of knowledge is anything but disinterested (151).

Just as "Tom Outland's Story" exposes the gap between Tom's subjective interpretations and the unknowable objective reality of the cultural "others" he is studying, so the first book of *The Professor's House*, "The Family," extends this epistemological problem, presenting the many attempts to grasp the objective reality of the absent Tom as similarly subjective interpretations of an unknowable "other." In the final book of the novel, "The Professor," this gap between subjective and objective knowledge, between self and "other," is turned inward as Professor St. Peter comes to see himself as "other." While externally concerned with annotating and introducing Tom's diary, the Professor finds himself internally engaged in daydreams of his own youthful self—"the original, unmodified Godfrey St. Peter" (239). His attempts to grasp the objective reality of this original self, what he calls the "realest of his lives" (240), leads him through a type of "reversion" so that his present life "seemed to him like the life of another person" (243).

Acknowledging the unbridgeable gap between his "original ego" and the "secondary social man" he has become, the Professor has come to view himself as "other" (239). As "other" he can never truly know himself, just as he feels he no longer knows his family, and so he seemingly acquiesces to death as the gas from the unlit stove fills his study. His rescue and recovery by the serving-woman Augusta leads not to a sense of salvation but to a "sense of obligation." The void within himself and the epistemological gap between himself and others remains, but he accepts his social bond with "a world full of Augustas, with whom one was outward bound" (257).

By the 1920s, Cather had moved away from the comparative method of *The Song of the Lark* toward a method she called juxtaposition: "to cut out all analysis, observation, description, even the picture-making quality, in order to make things and people tell their own story simply by juxtaposition, without any persuasion or explanation on my part" (*On Writing* 24). In *The Professor's House*, Cather's use of juxtaposition reveals the novel's concern with the epistemological problem of how one knows others and the external world. By juxtaposing "Tom Outland's Story" with the other two books of the novel, Cather seemingly allows Tom, the absent "other" of the novel, to reappear and tell his own story. Unlike the third-person point of view of the rest of the novel, which presents St. Peter as the central consciousness, Tom tells his own story in the first person. Glen A. Love suggests that the oral style of book 2 ("Tom Outland's Story"), with its simple sentences and monosyllabic words, distinguishes it from the complex sentences and "overfurnished" style of book 1 and the internalized, "primal" language of book 3 (301, 305). Cather thus seems to juxtapose Tom's story with the other books of the novel without providing any explanation or evaluation of the story. Yet the author undercuts the requirements of her method, as we have seen, by prefacing "Tom Outland's Story" with the evaluative interpretation of St. Peter: "It was nothing very incriminating, nothing very remarkable; a story of youthful defeat, the sort of thing a boy is sensitive about—until he grows older" (155). What we are thrown back upon again is the epistemological problem of the novel: we cannot grasp the objective reality of the absent "other," even when we apparently hear Tom's story told in his own words, because we are aware from the outset that the story is filtered through St. Peter's memory and framed by his subjective interpretations of Tom as a symbol of the idealism and desire of his own lost youth. Just as the absent cliff dwellers remain subject to Tom's (mis)interpretations, so the absent Tom remains subject to the (mis)interpretations of St. Peter. In both cases the "other" remains unknown.

In representing the epistemological conflict upon which cultural relativism is founded, Cather's novel anticipates recent critiques of the mode of ethnography associated with modern anthropology. As we have seen, Boas viewed different cultures as subjectively perceived wholes, and one of the concerns of cultural relativism was to salvage the artifacts of apparently "vanishing" tribes so that these cultures could be understood in their totality. Ethnographies were written most often in the mode of realism "to allude to a whole by means of parts or foci of analytical attention which constantly evoke a social and cultural totality" (Marcus and Fischer 23). While Boas understood the subjective foundation of interpretation, modern anthropological methods and realist ethnographies focused on the interpreted object, not the interpreting subject, adopting an objective viewpoint, "standpoint outside—looking at, objectifying, or somewhat closer, 'reading,' a given reality" (Clifford, "Introduction" 11). Contemporary anthropology offers an alternative view of culture and the position of the cultural interpreter through its use of discourse analysis, which views "culture" represented through ethnography as "relational, an inscription of communicative processes that exist historically, between subjects in relations of power" (Clifford, "Introduction" 15). Rather than an object of description, a self-contained and bordered totality, culture is now understood as a borderlands: "a more porous array of intersections where distinct processes crisscross from within and beyond its borders" (Rosaldo 20). Such distinct processes are dependent upon social differences and are subject to change, conflict, and resistance.

New methods of discourse analysis and new models of cultural borderlands require new forms of ethnography, polyvocal and non-totalizing forms of representation that inscribe or transcribe difference at the level of both content and form (Clifford, "Ethnographic" 104). While the method of juxtaposition evident in *The Professor's House* provides one mode of inscribing multiple "voices" and representing difference, as we have seen, the voice of the "other" remains either silenced or framed by subjective (mis)interpretations. Since the "other" (the cliff dwellers and Tom) remains absent, and the "interpreter" (Tom and St. Peter) does not recognize the subjective nature of his (mis)interpretations, true dialogism is impossible. There is never any real opportunity for cross-cultural dialogue or self-reflexive analysis of the discursive processes through which "others" are represented by and as historically situated subjects in specific relations of power. In essence, juxtaposition suggests a dialogic relation between distinct objects and persons through formal gaps within the text that seem to inscribe difference, yet the "other's" difference remains effaced: the "other" is present only as an object of knowledge but remains absent as a historically situated subject, and the subjective representations of the cultural interpreter, also a historically situated subject, remain self-reflexively unexamined.

Though published only two years after *The Professor's House*, *Death Comes for the Archbishop* offers a very different view of the cultures of the Southwest: a dialogic representation of a cultural borderlands peopled by historically situated subjects in specific relations of power. After finishing *The Professor's House*, Cather made two final trips to the Southwest in the summer of 1925 and 1926, during which she conceived and finalized her ideas for *Death Comes for the Archbishop* (Woodress 393). In *Death Comes for the Archbishop*, which Cather described as a "conjunction of the general and the particular" (*On Writing* 9), the story of the Catholic Church provides the author with a transcultural framework for writing about the disparate cultures and traditions she encountered in the Southwest. At the same time, Cather's own cross-cultural encounters on her last two trips to the Southwest provide another conjunctive framework, this one intercultural.

On her final two trips to the Southwest, Cather spent a great deal of time with Tony Luhan, the husband of Mabel Dodge Luhan and a tribal leader of the Tiwa pueblo. Edith Lewis, Cather's traveling companion during these trips, recalls that "Willa Cather was very impressed by Tony Luhan, and felt an instant liking and admiration for him" (142). He took them on long drives through the country and introduced them to aspects of both Native American and Mexican cultures:

Tony would sit in the driver's seat, in his silver bracelets and purple blanket, often singing softly to himself; while we sat behind. He took us to some of the almost inaccessible Mexican villages hidden in the Cimmaron mountains, where the Penitentes still followed their old fierce customs; and from Tony, Willa Cather learned many things about the country and the people that she could not have learned otherwise. He talked very little, but what he said was always illuminating and curiously poetic. (Lewis 142)

Lewis's description of Tony was in keeping with the traditional Indian image of him that his wife, Mabel, created for her white friends (fig. 11). Yet Tony was able "to negotiate two entirely different worlds and cultures with aplomb. . . . When white folk came knocking on his door in the hopes of receiving the age-old wisdom of the Indians, they were more than likely to get an earful about the automobiles he loved to drive" (Rudnick, *Utopian* 47). Still, Tony maintained political and cultural connections with his tribe:

Because intermarriage was forbidden by tribal law, Tony had to give up his participation in kiva ceremonies. He did, however, retain his position on the Tribal Council, the governing body made up of the heads of various societies that met to decide issues of importance to tribal welfare. (Rudnick, *Mabel* 155)

Furthermore, as a cultural leader of the Tiwa, who "were among the most secretive of the Pueblo tribes in terms of what they were allowed to reveal to outsiders" (Rudnick, *Mabel* 158), Tony was "vigilant about guarding pueblo secrets" (Rudnick, *Utopian* 95). Thus Tony provided Cather with an intercultural model of the dialogic social transactions that characterize the cultural borderlands.

In *Death Comes for the Archbishop*, Cather represents the Catholic Church as both a powerful force driving such intercultural negotiations and a transcultural form of social organization that fosters social unity while at the same time recognizing difference. I would argue that Cather's novel is "catholic" less in terms of the religious faith it espouses than in its attempt to encompass a multiplicity of worldviews, beliefs, and values. The project of the Catholic Church, which initiates both the novel and the project of future Archbishop Latour, is spiritual and political: to maintain the faith in the New World, expand the reach of the Catholic empire, and work with the "progressive government" of the United States to settle peacefully the new territory of its own expanded empire, annexed by conquest and the Treaty of Guadalupe Hidalgo (6–7). The man who can accomplish such a project "must be a man to whom order is necessary—as dear as life" (8), since he must find a way to control a diverse and often antagonistic population fragmented by different cultures and spiritual and political interests. Organizing the autonomous and differentially specific impulses of these various groups requires someone with "a sense of proportion and rational adjustment" who, like the artist of Cather's "Light on Adobe Walls," can "discover the logical relation of things" (9).

Death Comes for the Archbishop represents the borderlands of the Southwest as an intersection of different cultures understood not as fixed totalities but as social processes subject to change, conflict, and resistance. Following the intercultural model of Tony Luhan, Cather constructs certain characters who help to mediate between these distinct cultures and serve as sites for dialogic interaction. Father Vaillant, who is represented as a crosser of cultural boundaries, is able to disaffiliate himself from his own French culture in order to affiliate himself with the "native" communities he serves. Father Joseph, as Vaillant is referred to by others, continually refers to the Mexicans as "his own people" (257) and attempts to convince the Bishop that he (who no longer identifies himself as French) can serve the people better than a "French priest": "none of our new priests understand those poor natures as I do. I have almost become a Mexican! I have learned to like *chili colorado* and mutton fat. Their foolish ways no longer offend me, their faults are dear to me. I am *their man!*" (208, italics in original). Vaillant adapts not only to Mexican culture but to a variety of cultural contexts: "He added a glow to whatever kind of human society he was dropped down into. A Navajo hogan, some abjectly poor little huddle of Mexican huts, or a company of Monsignori and Cardinals at Rome— it was all the same" (227). The patronizing and, some might say, appropriative aspects of this white European missionary's intercultural enactments are balanced by the more reserved efforts of the Archbishop's Navajo friend Eusabio, whose character Cather may have modeled after Tony Luhan (Lewis 143). Eusabio serves as a sartorial model for the intercultural processes driven by Spanish imperialism under the banner of Roman Catholicism:

> He always dressed very elegantly in velvet and buckskin rich with bead and quill embroidery, belted with silver, and wore a blanket of the finest wool and design. His arms, under the loose sleeves of his shirt, were covered with silver bracelets, and on his breast hung very old necklaces of wampum and turquoise and coral—Mediterranean coral, that had been left in the Navajo country by Coronado's captains when they passed through it on their way to discover the Hopi villages and the Grand Canyon. (220)

Eusabio also reminds Latour that Native Americans have adapted to certain aspects of their new American colonizer's culture—for example, the railroad: at least to "travel faster now" if not to "go to better things" (289). Finally, it is Eusabio who attempts to mediate between the rebel Navajo leader Manuelito and the U.S. government persecuting his people by bringing Manuelito to speak with the Archbishop (292).

In addition to these cultural mediators, certain religious icons, rituals, and related practices also serve as sites for intercultural negotiations and transcultural connections. Latour recognizes the forces of religious empire that drive such processes when he describes to Father Vaillant the intercultural origins of his Angelus bell ("an adaptation of a Moslem custom") and the transcultural spread of silverworking skills: "The Spaniards handed on their skill to the Mexicans, and the Mexicans have taught the Navajos to work silver, but it all came from the Moors" (45). Latour himself learns from a Mexican priest how the Virgin Mary is indigenized in the New World as the intercultural figure of La Virgen de Guadalupe, the patron saint of Mexico (49). Similarly, a portrait of Saint Joseph serves as an icon in certain intercultural rituals at Ácoma and "never fails to produce rain" (87). Finally, the syncretic design of the church at Laguna, which is "painted above and about the altar with gods of wind and rain and thunder, sun and moon" (89), may serve as a model for Latour's cathedral, made of native yellow rock with a European design and which he desires to make an integral part of its setting (270).

Through the presentation of mediating figures and intercultural negotiations, Cather constructs a system of equivalences that connects the differentially specific cultural practices, values, and beliefs presented by the novel. This is not to say, however, that cultural differences are transcended. At times, the logic of difference, which emphasizes autonomous and distinct identities, asserts itself. Latour, unlike Tom Outland or Professor St. Peter, recognizes the epistemological gap that exists between self and "other." Thus he suggests that cultural differences may preclude the transfer of knowledge between him and his Pecos Indian guide, Jacinto:

> There was no way in which he could transfer his own memories of European civilization into the Indian mind, and he was quite willing to believe that behind Jacinto there was a long tradition, a story of experience, which no language could translate to him. (92)

Latour's sense of cultural "otherness" is nowhere more evident than in the Stone Lips episode, in which he descends with Jacinto into a sacred cave used for tribal rituals (including, he imagines, snake worship) and is left with feelings of "repugnance" and "horror" (133). However, he also recognizes that the stories of sacrificial snake worship he hears are merely used to rationalize the destruction of Native American cultures and that the specific relations of power and the historical conditions produced by Spanish and American colonization (including slavery and "contagious disease brought by white men") are the real causes of the decimated Indian populations (123). Likewise, Cather clearly articulates the differentially specific struggles of individual cultures against the forces of colonization: the rebellion of the Taos Indians, which may or may not have been instigated by the rebellious Mexican priest, Padre Martínez; the anti-Americanism of the "Spanish" aristocrat Don Manuel Chavez; the Mexican resistance to the American war of conquest; and the resistance of the Navajo leader, Manuelito, to violent displacement and extermination of his people at the hands of Kit Carson and the U.S. military. Thus the logic of difference, asserted throughout the novel, affirms the differentially specific cultural and historical contexts represented in the southwestern borderlands.

Anticipating the dialogic approach to culture of contemporary anthropology, Cather balances in her novel the logic of difference and the logic of equivalence, allowing for an examination of the discursive processes through which "others" are represented. In *On Writing*, Cather suggests that she sought an aesthetic form for her novel that would allow her to "do something in the style of legend," something like the frescoes of Puvis de Chavannes, "something without accent" (9). In order to write a story "without accent," she had to resist the temptation to make a certain incident "stand out too much, to particularize it" (12). She wanted "not to use an incident for all there is in it—but to touch and pass on" (9). For this form of writing, in which no incident was subordinated to any other, Cather preferred the term "narrative" rather than "novel," in which a series of events is arranged in a chronological and hierarchical sequence (12). Thus Cather asserts that a logic of equivalence governs her narrative: all the episodes are "of about the same importance" (9). Yet, as we have seen, in individual episodes a logic of difference is asserted, as differentially specific persons, objects, and incidents are represented within their historical context and in certain relations of power. In contrast to the cultural evolutionism of *The Song of the Lark*, in which distinct cultural manifestations are arranged into a singular, hierarchical sequence of progressive cultural development, and in contrast to the cultural relativism of *The Professor's House*, in which cultures are objectively viewed as self-contained and bordered totalities, in the cultural borderlands of *Death Comes for the Archbishop* cultures are constructed through a process of intercultural mediation and negotiation, which allows for self-reflexive analysis of the discursive processes through which "others" are represented by and as historically situated subjects in specific relations of power.

In some recent criticism, Cather's writing of culture has been characterized as a form of racism. According to this argument, "the persistence of race marks the point beyond which no transformation is possible" (Michaels, *Our America* 78) for Cather, and thus "Cather's racism and ethnocentricity undercut her attempt to create art somehow outside of or at least in dialog with inherited, conventional, white western narrative tradition" (Ammons 134). However, Cather's approach to the concept of culture was not dependent upon a fixed and essentialist notion of race. Her understanding of culture underwent numerous changes in response to her readings in archaeology and anthropology and to her personal encounters with the peoples of the Southwest. Moreover, these developments in her understanding of culture (theories I have referred to as cultural evolutionism, cultural relativism, and cultural borderlands) corresponded to developments in her aesthetic practices (methods I have described as comparison, juxtaposition, and dialogism). By developing new approaches to the writing of culture, new ways of representing the "relation of creatures or objects to each other," Cather was able to move beyond the conventional narrative form of *The Song of the Lark* and toward the experimental narrative techniques of *The Professor's House* and *Death Comes for the Archbishop*.

Manuel Broncano

Landscapes of the Magical

Cather's and Anaya's Explorations of the Southwest

The American experience involves a peculiar conception of land and self. Since the discovery of America as a result of Christopher Columbus's miscalculation, the New World has been tinged with the uncanny and the mysterious. Reports sent to Europe by conquistadores and colonizers of all kinds described a landscape where the fabulous and the real mingled together, a sort of mythological region where every wonder seemed possible. From the beginning, America has been subject to utter misrepresentation, both in the European mind and in the minds of all those adventurers who came to the shores of the New World and then pushed farther and farther into the wilderness in search of a chimera of success and regeneration. In the history of early America, contradictory discourses speak of epic deeds and deplorable failures, always in the guise of a Christian and civilizing mission, or a divine "errand into the wilderness." On the one hand, Hernán Cortés and his squalid battalion of fearless mercenaries conquer the fabulous empire of the Aztecs, backed by the devil-like power of horses and armor; on the other hand, Cabeza de Vaca rambles for ten years on the plains and deserts of the Southwest, the object of trade and abuse among Indians of numerous tribes, and becomes a shaman, or holy man, performing a number of obscure "miraculous healings." Radically different in their tone and content, the reports sent back to Charles I of Spain by Cortés and de Vaca articulate distorted perceptions of the reality they confronted. Yet Cortés's discourse of "mythification" and de Vaca's discourse of "demythification," or failure, coincide in projecting a vision of the New World as a region of wonders and mysteries. American writers of all regions have since developed an acute eye for the "strangeness" of our everyday world and the ambiguous texture of the reality we inhabit.

One striking inheritor of the American tradition of "strangeness" is the remarkable phenomenon in contemporary Hispanic fiction labeled "magical realism." The term has been most often used in relation to the Latin American boom of Gabriel García Márquez, Juan Rulfo, Carlos Fuentes, and others. Notorious disagreement exists, however, over its extent and meaning, making it difficult to use as a general category of analysis. It has been less frequently applied to the dominant literature of the United States, where, nonetheless, realistic writing has always shown a conspicuous tendency toward the magical and the romantic. Thus, Hawthorne and his contemporaries wrote *romances*, a peculiar kind of realism that tries to reveal the mysteries of everyday reality. And even in the novel that represents the summit of American realism, *The Adventures of Huckleberry Finn*, there is a clear presence of the magical (for example, Jim's superstitions and the fear they inspire in Huck), besides a romantic and transcendental vein that permeates the text. In Twain's novel, moreover, frontier humor softens the violent and tense situations that abound in Huck and Jim's journey: a kind of humor characteristic of magical realism as practiced by García Márquez and others. We should also remember the great influence that William Faulkner has exerted on the writers of the Latin American boom, who in return have provided a literary model quite influential in contemporary American fiction.

The debate over the nature and influence of magical realism is extensive. Enrique Anderson Imbert was the first to attempt a distinction between magical realism and the fantastic; Tzvetan Todorov established the distinction between the fantastic and the marvelous; Lucia I. Mena equated the magico-realist mode to Todorov's sense of the marvelous and concluded that while the fantastic creates mysteries that are outside our world, magical realism seeks mysteries that are part of reality. To Mena, the mysterious and the supernatural do not collide with the real but become part of it (66). Roland Walter has suggested that magical realism shows three characteristics: (1) the existence of two levels of reality—the real and the magical; (2) the harmonious integration of the two levels of reality; and (3) a reduced authorial instance, or a reticence on the part of the author (and the narrator) to provide rational explanations regarding magical events. The magical view implies that the individual interprets reality not only in rational terms but also through the myths, legends, and superstitions inherited from the past. The result is that unreal, mysterious, and strange phenomena are perceived as real or natural. In the magico-realist mode, things and events are magical because the author, the narrator, and/or the characters perceive them as such by means of imagination (Walter 20–21).

The importance of magical realism as a category of analysis in the context of North America has been the focus of pioneer critical exercises in the field. José D. Saldivar, whose "Postmodern Realism" in the *Columbia Literary History of the American Novel* (1991) confirms magical realism as a pan-American phenomenon deeply ingrained in the peculiarities of society and history in the New World, identifies practitioners as Toni Morrison, Arturo Islas, Maxine Hong Kingston, and other U.S. writers whose practice of the mode has received "little attention in our largely Anglophonic Departments of Literature, owing to an inadequate understanding of a vast and rich literary and cultural movement in the Americas that began over forty years ago" (523). Lois P. Zamora (1995) shares Saldivar's transnational approach to the mode, pointing out its proximity to the grotesque in its capacity for unsettling the reader and provoking disgust, a relation to which we shall return later. Wayne Ude (1981, 1989) has identified magical realism as inherent to the North American literary tradition; his work provides the theoretical lead underlying this essay. For Ude, magical realism made its entrance as such in the United States in the late 1960s, in a postmodernist attempt at revitalizing the exhaustion of self-reflexive and language-centered fiction. The roots of the mode, however, extend back to the Puritans and their peculiar conceptions of civilization and wilderness, through the nineteenth-century romance-novel of Hawthorne and others, and up to what Ude labels "North American Magical Realism" ("Forging" 50). It is the purpose of this essay to demonstrate that Rudolfo Anaya and Willa Cather belong in that school as well, for they both practice the "magical grotesque" as the only viable representational mode for coping with the complex reality of the American Southwest.

The Southwest is unique in both the United States and the Americas at large, as it is a composite of peoples, civilizations, religions, and myths resulting from successive frontier experiences of cultural collision. The Southwest contains a landscape—physical and human—without referents in any other region. Confined in its sierras and mesas, gorges and deserts, rivers and valleys, convents and pueblos, it is a world of features to be found nowhere else on the continent. As a place where magic and legend permeate the beliefs and daily life of its inhabitants, this landscape seems to lie beyond the reach of the rational mind. This is, at least, the world created by the two New Mexico novels I will explore in this essay. Anaya's *Bless Me, Ultima* (originally published in 1972) is a bildungsroman about a child who awakes to the realities and mysteries of life. Cather's *Death Comes for the Archbishop* (1927) speaks of the encounter between a French priest and the region's very particular practice of Roman Catholicism. The two novels question the viability of Christian orthodoxy in the New World, while projecting the profound religious feelings of the population. They share, to varying degrees, a magical perspective on reality and a profound indebtedness to the aesthetics of the grotesque.

Bless Me, Ultima signals the coming-of-age of Chicano fiction in the American literary tradition. Anaya's novel is a song to a bygone era of tradition and folklore, but it is also a vindication of a culture that strives to preserve its essence in a world of increasing uniformity. In it, patterns and motifs of European origin are blended with indigenous belief, folk legend, myth, and poetically crafted scenes of local color (R. Saldívar 104). The result is an allegorical narrative that has been defined as a romance (Calderón 22) in an attempt to explain its generic ambiguity. In this sense, Anaya belongs to a long tradition in American letters, and his indebtedness to Hawthorne is evident. (The atmosphere of twentieth-century Guadalupe—the location of *Bless Me, Ultima*—closely resembles that of Puritan Boston or Salem as created by the New England writer.) For Roberto Cantú(1973), the novel possesses rich allegorical implications of place, and though it is set at a specific historical moment, its ultimate meaning is universal, for it deals with the archetypal struggle between good and evil. Other critics, like Jane Rogers (1986), have pointed to rich echoes of world mythology present in the novel, from the *Odyssey* to the Bible, as well as to myths that incorporate Mexican and Native American traditions and beliefs, such as the legend of La Llorona about a wailing woman who seeks her children, whom she has murdered, in rivers and lakes.

Ultima—the "good witch" who protects the young narrator Antonio in his passage to maturity—is vaguely characterized throughout the novel as possessing an ancient knowledge that escapes the reach of the contemporary mind. This wisdom helps her cure the diseases of body and soul and is the source of her understanding of events that appear "magical" to the rest of the characters. The very nature of magic is one of the central themes of the text, a concept whose meaning has been clearly subverted by the end of the narrative. In a passage resembling Jean Latour's famous perception of miracles as moments of refined perception, Antonio realizes the essence of the magical deeds he has seen performed by Ultima so many times: "Ultima has sympathy for people, and it is so complete that with it she can touch their souls and cure them. . . . That is her magic" (248).

The old Mexican woman thus becomes the embodiment of a Christlike archetype, while Antonio becomes her archetypal disciple whose task is to spread her message throughout the world. Ultima—called La Grande out of respect—is the last representative of her kind, as her name indicates. With her death, a way of life and a mode of understanding existence seem to disappear forever, except for the act of remembrance that is Antonio's written narrative, which recovers for an instant the ancient inheritance of Ultima's wisdom. She is the link between opposing worlds that seek harmony and quietude, the connection resolving irreconcilable dichotomies: day and night, reality and magic, Christianity and Indian religion, the Anglo-Saxon and the mestizo, good and evil, the farm and the llano, the past and the present, Christ and the golden carp, New Mexico and the world at large. Antonio is called to witness and reconcile these oppositions in his writing and thus become a "true" priest whose gospel speaks of convergence and reunion.

The same wish for preserving remembrance inspires Cather's *Death Comes for the Archbishop*. Again, we find the contrast between country and pueblo, the Anglo-Saxon and the mestizo, the rational and the uncanny (or miraculous), Christ and the primeval gods of the Indians, the desert and the farm. And again, in the background we hear the echoes of large historical forces: in Cather's novel it is the great American expansion to the West, while in Anaya's it is World War II and its impact on New Mexico. Both texts question the concept of history itself, which, like reality and reason, possesses limited relevance to a land unwilling to give up its myth and its magic. The landscape becomes the true protagonist in these novels, a region of wonders and mysteries, like the cave where Latour and his native companion seek shelter, a sanctuary of ancestral Indian rites where the French priest is forced to spend the night. This cave, known only to the Indians, has the shape of a mouth (it is called Stone Lips) and is connected to the heart of the earth and its unfathomable secrets. Here Latour has the intuition that Native beliefs and religious practices may be more than just a set of pagan superstitions, an intuition that forever transforms his perception of the Indians.

Father Latour's early encounter with the hostile geography of the Southwest, where a host of trials repeatedly test both his physical and spiritual strength, is even more painfully dramatic than the hardships anticipated by

Bishop Ferrand at the Vatican. As the carrier of civilization, the porter of the European mind, Latour attempts a task even more titanic than Antonio's preservation of tradition: to refuel orthodox Roman Catholicism in a land where Christian religion has mingled with Indian beliefs and practices and where the church has been converted into a system of personal and political power. On his first journey into the wilderness of New Mexico, Latour is the victim of his inability to recognize a country whose major feature is precisely that of being featureless (17). Dangerously lost in the desert, he finds his feet guided by a superior will that delivers him safely to an idyllic haven of water and vegetation, Agua Secreta, where he is welcomed by a group of Mexican settlers eager to receive the holy sacraments. The catalyst for this "miraculous" rescue is a specific act of self-surrender and sympathy in which Father Latour encounters a juniper tree with the exact form of the Cross. There he reenacts Christ's suffering in the Golgotha until his and Christ's flesh become indistinguishable. This paradigmatic early scene anticipates a series of "miracles"—events for which there is no plausible, rational explanation—witnessed by Latour and his lifelong companion, Father Joseph Vaillant, events that defy Latour's skeptic rationality and that gradually change his perception of reality and life. His is a long process of learning and understanding, until he realizes and accepts that there are things that go beyond reason, at least for the European mind he represents: "He was already convinced that neither the white men nor the Mexicans in Santa Fé understood anything about Indian beliefs or the workings of the Indian mind" (133). This recognition is but one instance of what I would call "ideological surrender," the transformation of a European in a New World that appears even older than the Old.

Cather's novel re-creates a magical atmosphere where diverse beliefs and superstitions converge, an atmosphere that openly defies narrow rationality. For Evelyn H. Hively, *Death Comes for the Archbishop* represents a study in comparative mythology: even though the protagonists are Roman Catholic priests, their archetypal experience is quite close to the Navajo myth of the Twin Heroes, who follow the holy trail, have as their father the sun, and are helped by the Indian counterpart to the Christian Virgin (157). Marilyn B. Callander, on the other hand, relates this pattern to a fairy-tale motif: the story of two brothers of opposite nature who set out in search of fortune. Along the way they find magic helpers (often animals or plants), confront dangers, and eventually become separated, until in the end they are reunited through the intervention of a magic object (50). Similarly, in *Death Comes for the Archbishop* different traditions come together and are reconciled, both Oriental and Occidental, European and Native. The bell of San Miguel, founded in the Spain of the Reconquest and then carried to America, is a symbol of the perfect continuity between the Orient and the Occident and between these and the New World: "I am glad to think there is Moorish silver in your bell," Latour tells Vaillant. "When we first came here, the one good workman we found in Santa Fé was a silversmith. The Spaniards handed on their skills to the Mexicans, and the Mexicans have taught the Navajos to work silver; but it all came from the Moors" (45).

The religion that emerges from *Death Comes for the Archbishop* is syncretic, alien to orthodoxy, like the altar decorated with the gods of the wind, the sun, the moon, and the rain, or the bell itself—a Catholic inheritance from the Moslems—or the painting of Saint Joseph that the natives use for their rainmaking rituals. The result is a landscape of fluid boundaries where the extraordinary becomes the norm and therefore ceases to be extraordinary. And this is, precisely, one of the basic features of the magic mode. In this landscape, animals and plants are often endowed with consequential intelligence. The symbiosis of humans and animals is present throughout the novel, a relation of interdependence where men sometimes prove to be the less intelligent (as in, for instance, Latour's guilt in the opening pages when "he, supposed to be the intelligence of the party, had got the poor animals into this interminable desert of ovens" [20]). The novel's bestiary includes a long list of species— cats, parrots, lizards, serpents, horses, donkeys, mules, and pigeons—that contribute to the creation of the text's pervasive magical atmosphere. On his first visit to Ácoma, Father Latour is struck by the turtlelike appearance of the natives: antediluvian-looking creatures of the sea that found refuge on the sun-baked top of the mesa. Sky City and its counterpart, the Enchanted Mesa, are the habitation of beings halfway between humans and animals, creatures in transition who, like the land itself, were left unfinished by God on the eve of creation: a "country . . . still waiting to be made into landscape" (95).

Cather's attention to plants and animals underscores the fundamental importance of organic nature to the discovered New World landscape of coalescence and interrelationship. *Death Comes for the Archbishop* is articulated upon a series of gardens that provide the text with a unifying structure, from the aristocratic garden in Rome at the beginning of the narrative, through the minutely re-created southwestern ecosystem, to the orchard where Jean Latour seeks refuge after retirement. Plants and trees are living forces that have adapted to the extreme conditions in that country and have become symbols of the life that flourishes there. The cruciform juniper tree under which Father Latour has a mystical experience, the tamarisk that protects under its shade every Mexican farm, the cacti that feed Manuel Chavez after his miraculous escape from the Indians, and the lavish vegetation in Agua Secreta are only a few examples of the profusion of vegetal life in the novel. Soon after Latour and Vaillant arrive in Santa Fe, they plant a garden that will grow old with them, its trees providing saplings for orchards all over the territory. The Archbishop spends his last years at the farm he bought from an old Mexican. There he puts his creative energy into landscaping and succeeds in domesticating native wildflowers with which he covers the land with a purple mantle, "the true Episcopal colour and countless variations of it" (265). Father Vaillant also insists on planting wherever he goes, from the shores of Lake Ontario to the gardens he creates in New Mexico and Colorado (a place where "nobody would stick a shovel in the earth for less than gold" [258]). This quiet labor, perhaps more lasting than evangelizing itself, leaves behind the priests a trail of vegetation, havens of life in the barren landscapes of the New World. Such a fusion of missionary work with gardening reunites land and spirit, self and nature.

Anaya's *Bless Me, Ultima* uses vegetal and animal life as the basic ingredients of magic. The novel is populated by primeval creatures that play a central role in human affairs. The most conspicuous example is Ultima's owl, the alter ego of the *curandera*: "the protective spirit of Ultima, the spirit of the night and the moon, the spirit of the llano! The Owl was her soul" (255). Ultima's owl deploys a power beyond human understanding and becomes the old woman's magical helper in her fight against evil. If the owl is the watcher of the air, the water is the kingdom of the golden carp, the true embodiment of an ancient Indian god. The golden carp, whose counterpart is the sinister black bass, is itself the pagan counterpart of Christ (R. Saldivar 114). Beyond that, even the river seems animated by a silent "presence" that teaches the young boy that his spirit "shared in the spirit of all things" (16). Vegetal life seems to be endowed with a soul: "For Ultima, even the plants had a spirit, and before I dug she made me speak to the plant and tell it why I pulled it from its home in the earth" (38). The motif of the garden recurs also in the text. Antonio's mother insists on farming the poor soil of their plot by the llano even though the crops they obtain are ridiculous. It is in her blood. Likewise, Narciso, the town drunkard who gives his life in an attempt to save Ultima, is endowed with a magical gift for farming, his orchard like the garden of Eden in its wealth and abundance. Narciso's garden, which he plants by moonlight while he dances, becomes a metonymy of himself: "The garden is like Narciso, it is drunk" (109). Here, as in Cather's novel, the communion of humans with animals and plants is complete, and the primeval wilderness of the Southwest emerges a space of kindred creatures, an organic unity of transcendental life where man's is but a humble lot. Only evil, in the form of Tenorio and Buck Scales, is capable of altering the essential harmony of this pastoral landscape. In the end, though, order is restored through the intervention of a superior force, such as Ultima and her owl or Latour and Vaillant under the protection of the Virgin.

Criticism of *Death Comes for the Archbishop* has explored in detail Cather's sources for the novel: Puvis de Chavannes's frescoes of the life of St. Geneviève, Holbein's *Dance of Death*, and Jacobus de Voragine's *The Golden Legend*. Cather was clearly turning her eyes back to the Middle Ages in search of aesthetic models. But critics have generally let pass without comment the presence in the text of the grotesque, a dominant mode in medieval art and literature. Anne Mosely (1998) has broken new ground with her study of Cather's conscious use of the grotesque in *My Mortal Enemy*. For Mosely, Cather's grotesque in that novel is essentially spiritual—in the sense that Flannery O'Connor defined and practiced it—and intends to portray the life of Myra Henshawe as "under construction," "involved in a transformative, regenerative spiritual process" (36). The essential quality of the grotesque, following Bakhtin's theory of carnival, is ambivalence: it re-creates a world of violent contrasts where differences between contraries are blurred and erased (Mosely 38). Cather's aesthetics, which embraced an admiration of Gothic cathedrals as well as a keen eye for the bizarre, converged in the grotesque as the mode that best suited her artistic concerns and expressed her awareness of the essential "deformity" of human society.

The grotesque is a mode akin to magical realism. Some critics even suggest that they are part of the same phenomenon. John R. Clark (1991), for example, names García Márquez's *One Hundred Years of Solitude*, a canonical text in magical realism, as representative of the "contemporary grotesque." David K. Danow (1995) has explored the proximity of the grotesque and the magical, finding in each expressions of the Bakhtinian carnivalesque attitude, a mode that has dominated twentieth-century art and literature. Henry Ziomek (1983) states that grotesque literature is the product of the interaction of two opposed sides of human nature and that it represents the search for the sublime through the perverse in a fusion of the tragic and the comic. The triple effect of this fusion process where the painful and the risible intermingle, conveying a bizarre effect, is horror, fear, and astonishment (Ziomek 14). The grotesque and the magical share ultimate goals of defying established institutions and habits, questioning and undoing inherited assumptions and fears, and helping human beings to accept their tragicomic destiny with a festive attitude. The Holbein engravings that inspired the title *Death Comes for the Archbishop* are a good illustration, as they depict deformed beings (like many of the characters in Cather's novel) who pullulate in a landscape of grotesque excess. Cather's Trinidad Lucero, for example, is a caricature of his progenitors, an exaggeration of their lowliness and vice, and his ordination as a priest in the schismatic church represents a carnivalesque parody of the most sacred rites of Roman Catholicism. The spurious descendant of a race that has degenerated for centuries in the spiritual and geographic isolation of the Southwest, the young Lucero—lacking a moral sense to guide him— confuses the holy and the profane. Thus, in accordance with a basic trait of the grotesque, he becomes the symbol of the enormous gap between the foundational ideals of the church and the reality of the heterodox Roman Catholicism that has flourished in the New World.

Human and nonhuman life-forms, animal and vegetal, proliferate and intermingle in *Death Comes for the Archbishop*. And the landscape itself, which I have defined as a landscape of excesses, is out of all measure, like the desert of ovens in which Latour gets lost at the beginning of the narrative. Yet probably the novel's most grotesque quality is the duality or duplicity of the icons and symbols that abound in the text. Gardens, for example, can be places of ecstatic vision, as in the scene where Magdalena appears transfigured among the pigeons (209); but they can also be the cause of human perdition, as for Father Baltazar, who gives up the idea of running away because his orchard is at its prime (110–11). Pascal's double-edged dictum, as quoted by Latour ("man was lost and saved in a garden" [265]), seems verified by the facts of the novel. The snake, which for the Archbishop is a symbol of evil, is for the natives a symbol of life and nature. The goat, a figure of pagan lasciviousness in Christian iconography, provides humans with warmth and nourishment. ("The young bishop smiled at his mixed theology. But though the goat had always been the symbol of pagan lewdness, he told himself that their fleece had warmed many a good Christian, and their rich milk nourished sickly children" [31].) The cathedral itself, a cultural aberration in the landscape of New Mexico, represents the perfect, although shocking, melting of opposed cultural traditions. In this respect, Latour's midi-Romanesque church becomes the supreme symbol into which all the essential dichotomies framing the narrative are dissolved. It is a monument to convergence and reunion, a symbol of the reconciliation between contraries. The cathedral represents a new creature, "beautiful in its deformity" (Mosely 35) born out of the soil of the New World yet deeply rooted in the Old. The building is Latour's desperate attempt to remain faithful to European orthodoxy, but the bishop and the tradition he embodies inevitably undergo a radical transformation in the new land. Such transformation is, precisely, the essential drive of the grotesque.

In *Bless Me, Ultima* we find a similar carnivalization of Catholic rites, whose solemnity is derided by the irreverence of youth. Antonio's life during the year re-created in the novel is a long preparation for his first communion, a time of fears and questions without answers. When the ceremony finally arrives, however, the ritual's high seriousness is comically desecrated by the irreverent attitude of the young communicants, and the wafer fails to provide Antonio with the reassurance he had so eagerly expected (221). The Catholic rite does not fulfill his expectations of a sudden knowledge of God: only when the golden carp and Ultima's "gospel" find their place next to Jesus in the heart of the boy is he capable of grasping the true nature of divinity. His is the pantheistic perception of a divine being inherent in all extant creatures. The world of radical dichotomies thus gives way to the essential unity of creation, something still emergent, as in Cather's novel: "Take the llano and the river valley, the moon and the sea, God and the golden carp—and make something new" (147). This is Ultima's call to the boy: create anew a world of order and harmony out of the material of chaos; complete the landscape left unfinished by God, as Father Latour once thought of the Ácoma country.

Cather said that she considered *Death Comes for the Archbishop* her best novel. On another occasion she declared that it was hardly a novel and said she preferred to call it a "narrative" in an attempt to explain its generic peculiarities. The book is her aesthetic response to the Southwest, a region where she underwent a profound artistic and personal transformation. Like many of her fictional characters, Cather was faced with the "great fact" of the land itself. And the encounter proved fruitful. In New Mexico, Cather found life in its primary essence, a self-contained universe older than creation, and she learned to translate it into fiction. Inevitably, her writing entered the realm of the "magical grotesque," for it is the mode native to that soil—

the same soil that nourishes Anaya's *Bless Me, Ultima*, the moving portrait of a vanishing world threatened by the general uniformity of contemporary America. Despite their cultural, racial, and ideological differences, Cather and Anaya emerge as kindred artists whose portrayals of the Southwest have provided literature with one of its most intriguing regions. We ought to place that region next to Macondo, Yoknapatawpha, or la Mancha in the fictional geography of our world.

Joseph R. Urgo

Multiculturalism as Nostalgia in Cather, Faulkner, and U.S. Culture

An observation made by J. Hector St. John de Crevecoeur, that in America "individuals of all nations are melted into a new race of men, whose labours and posterity will one day cause great changes in the world" (70), was as prophetic in 1782 as it is troubling today. What of difference? What of the integrity of cultures? Crevecoeur predicted that difference would be supplanted by *indifference*, particularly regarding what was the most divisive social distinction of his time, religious sectarianism. In America, Crevecoeur explains,

> all sects are mixed, . . . as well as all nations; thus religious indifference
> is imperceptibly disseminated from one end of the continent to the
> other, which is at present one of the strongest characteristics of the
> Americans. Where this will reach no one can tell.

"Perhaps it will lead to a vacuum fit to receive other systems," Crevecoeur muses (76). Religious and ethnic indifference continue to mark U.S. culture, but that indifference has also led to another system of thought, one that reacts strongly to indifference and seeks to maintain, or to resurrect, those distinctions that democratic indifference devalues. The current emanation to emerge from the vacuum of indifference is multiculturalism, which might be understood as something like an *advance nostalgia* for qualities destined to become irrelevant in the United States. The famous lament by Henry David Thoreau echoes across the centuries in America: "They force me to become like themselves. I do not hear of *men* being *forced* to live this way or that by masses of men. What sort of life were that to live?" (403). It is an American sort of life, where the distinctions of culture are made irrelevant not only through the indifference of the state but by the leveling habits of its citizenry, and material rewards go to those who become indifferent—or tolerant—as well.

A seeming oxymoron, *advance nostalgia* condenses a historical process and an ideological prerequisite. The process works this way: the particular ethnic identity is granted entry into the United States, sometimes through labor recruitment, sometimes by falling within immigration quotas. Based upon that status, certain stipulations or privileges may be conferred, such as visa limitations or affirmative action assistance. However, long-term acceptance into the culture—specifically, into middle-class, consumer, and corporate culture—requires the gradual loosening of the original ethnic identity (language, clothing, religious practices, family structure) and the assumption of various standard Americanisms. Faced with the feared dissolution of origins, a nostalgia for what is to be lost precedes its actual dissolution, and various forms of cultural assertiveness result. These cultural forms, known aggregately as multiculturalism, are attempts to maintain difference within an ideology of indifference. Thus, in any given year, in my old hometown of Cranston, Rhode Island, one could attend the African American celebration in January, the Irish parade in March, the Hispanic fiesta in April, Southeast Asian days in May, the Italian feast in August, the Greek festival in September, the Armenian celebration in October. July, though, is reserved for the Declaration of Indifference—that is to say, Independence. These ethnic events do not look like funerals, but that is what they are: eulogistic celebrations of lost identities meant to keep alive the memory of what was sacrificed to the new belief, America. These events originate in *advance nostalgia*, established by immigrant groups experiencing the pull of indifference and relegating their heritage to its acceptable place in the United States: as potentially profitable, politically expedient, entertainment.

Two of the more famous characters in twentieth-century American literature are Jean Latour, the missionary priest in Willa Cather's 1927 novel, *Death Comes for the Archbishop*, and Isaac McCaslin, the "uncle to half a county" in William Faulkner's *Go Down, Moses*, published in 1942. The two men lead very different lives, but each wrestles with the fundamental American dilemma of how to contemplate difference. The Archbishop's great desire is to build a Romanesque cathedral in the American Southwest and bring to the multitudinous variety of faiths and beliefs in existence in the region the universalizing mission of Roman Catholicism. However, Archbishop Latour discovers that some differences among peoples are immutable, and thus the universalizing mission of the Catholic Church—a potential metaphor for the universalizing, or leveling, tendencies of American society—is thwarted by the intransigence of indigenous cultures. Specifically, the Archbishop builds his cathedral, but its magnificence is haunted by its failure to incorporate Native American beliefs into its Roman Catholicism.

In an important scene, Latour is with his guide, Jacinto, a Native American man and a member of the Laguna tribe, who explains certain Laguna beliefs to the priest. The Archbishop's thoughtfully frustrated response signals New World panic at the prospect that indifference might prove less powerful than difference.

> The two companions sat, each thinking his own thoughts as night closed in about them; a blue night set with stars, the bulk of the solitary mesas cutting into the firmament. The Bishop seldom questioned Jacinto about his thoughts or beliefs. He didn't think it polite, and he believed it to be useless. There was no way in which he could transfer his own memories of European civilization into the Indian mind, and he was quite willing to believe that behind Jacinto there was a long tradition, a story of experience, which no language could translate to him. A chill came with the darkness. Father Latour put on his old, fur-lined cloak, and Jacinto, loosening the blanket tied about his loins, drew it up over his head and shoulders. (92)

We might identify that chill as the chill of insurmountable human difference, of distinctions hardened into rock which even the heat of living bodies cannot transcend. The experience tires Archbishop Latour and stands as a qualification of some magnitude to the universalizing faith of his calling. It brings to mind Chief Seattle's controversial 1855 statement: "Your God is not our God! Your God loves your people and hates mine. . . . We are two distinct races with separate origins and separate destinies. There is little in common between us" (227–28).

Militating against despair, however, is Cather's own strong language of potentiality, where she claims that despite centuries of inhabitation, the Southwest had yet to take the form of a comprehensive location.

> The mesa plain had an appearance of great antiquity, and of incompleteness; as if, with all the materials for world-making assembled, the Creator had desisted, gone away and left everything on the point of being brought together, on the eve of being arranged into mountain, plain, plateau. The country was still waiting to be made into a landscape. (94–95)

A major part of that landscape—the human part—will be the construction of

Father Latour's cathedral. "The cathedral is very near to my heart, for many reasons" (242–43), Latour explains to his fellow priest—not least of which, I would venture to say, is the establishment of a landscape on which history might commence. It is a familiar story on the U.S. frontier: for American civilization to take root, insurmountable human differences must be set back into the dust. On this landscape, Cather's language of potentiality merges with Latour's Roman Catholicism, producing the long view of history thoroughly embedded in the novel.

In *Go Down, Moses* Isaac McCaslin spends less time than Father Latour reading landscape and more time contemplating the historical record to determine how his vision may influence or reform institutions of human behavior. The landscape on which Faulkner's character exists is thick with the record of entangled experiences: the footprints of forebears are chronicled in the language of commerce in the ledger books held in the tenant farm commissary. Unlike the world of Father Latour, in Isaac McCaslin's America it is not difference that astonishes but the depth of connection, the entanglement of human lives through the sexual, economic, and social exchanges of indifference.

> As a child and even after nine and ten and eleven, when he had learned to read, he would look up at the scarred and cracked backs and ends [of the ledger books] but with no particular desire to open them, and though he intended to examine them someday because he realised that they probably contained a chronological and much more comprehensive though doubtless tedious record than he would ever get from any other source, not alone of his own flesh and blood but of all his people, not only the whites but the black one too, who were as much a part of his ancestry as his white progenitors, and of the land which they had all held and used in common and fed from and on and would continue to use in common without regard to color or titular ownership. (256)

Whereas Father Latour knows there are differences between himself and the peoples of the Southwest and fears those differences are immutable, Isaac knows a commonality between whites and blacks on his land and discovers, when he finally reads the ledgers, the full and tragic implications of those genetic links to "not only the whites but the black" line as well.

Isaac McCaslin seeks to transcend difference in the name of what we would call today "common ground"; his triumph is in his own transcription of allegiance—memory, belief, and value—from his white inheritance to ideas learned from Native American traditions. Isaac does what Archbishop Latour says is impossible: he *transfers* the memories and experiences of another race into his consciousness when he accepts Sam Fathers as his ancestor. He ceases to identify himself with the culture of his heritage—his bloodline— and assumes affinity with a cultural tradition represented by the Native American hunter. When he has his vision of the buck, he leaves Christianity and enters the pantheistic world of Sam Fathers. Latour, on the other hand, becomes more convinced as he grows older that "The Mexicans were always Mexicans, the Indians were always Indians" (284) and that such transference was exceedingly difficult to accomplish. Despite his efforts, he fears that the rock of such distinctions was made of harder stuff than the rock bestowed by Christ on St. Peter, the universality of the human spirit.

Nonetheless, the Archbishop's vision of universality, his *faith* in transcendence, is very strong and, even when he fails, fires his imagination and provides him the strength to continue to attempt the impossible in America. Asleep in Santa Fe, Father Latour hears the nine o'clock Angelus bell and experiences "a pleasing delusion that he was in Rome." Before the nine bells have sounded, "Rome faded, and behind it he sensed something Eastern," which may be his imagination of Jerusalem, "though he had never been there." The sound of the Angelus bell "had carried him farther and faster than sound could travel" (43). Cather is profoundly ironic to set her narrative of American universalism among Catholic missionaries in the Southwest. The American dream of transcendence—to overpass national, geographic, and religious origins and achieve *e pluribus unum*, "from many, one"—may be imagined as a kind of secular Catholicism, demanding a faith no less strong than Father Latour's to accomplish. Only partially conscious, in an out-of-body, spiritual experience, Latour can be taken anywhere by the sound of the Angelus— Rome, Jerusalem, New Orleans, France—and he would still be *here*, in his partial consciousness, as the American bishop, the universalist. It is clear that despite the Archbishop's experience of difference, his belief—his *faith*— remains universal, Catholic. The conclusions he draws about the seemingly immutable nature of the cultural traditions that manifest through human life are failures of the flesh, not the spirit.

Isaac McCaslin believes also in a universalism, but that belief places him at odds with his time and place in Mississippi in the 1940s. The transference he makes spiritually, with Sam Fathers, precedes him, in the ledger books, in the generational and familial transactions between the white and blacks on the McCaslin-Edmonds-Beauchamp plantation. He stands his ground until, near the end of his life, like Latour, he realizes that the dream of universalism held implications that even he could not accept. "He had been asleep" (338), Faulkner narrates. It is the moment when Ike confronts the possibility that the racial division between blacks and whites, as well as the hierarchies of bloodlines that intersect among the white McCaslins and their black cousins, the Beauchamps, may be untenable; that the differences are false in *actuality* as well as in theory, or belief. (The scene is in "Delta Autumn" where Isaac encounters the child, the male heir to the plantation, fathered by Roth Edmonds and his distant, "black" Beauchamp cousin.) However, faced with the possibility that his transcendent, universalist beliefs may become flesh, Isaac panics. "*Maybe in a thousand or two thousand years in America he thought. But not now!*" (344). Isaac's defensive long view is, ironically, quite Catholic, reminiscent of the historical vision held by the cardinals at the Vatican, who open *Death Comes for the Archbishop* perched upon a shelf of rock, overlooking the hills of Rome. In both novels, then, there is a vision of universalism. In *Go Down, Moses*, that vision is set at odds with a social order that demands the maintenance of racial distinction, and it ultimately fails when the one human being who can see it loses sight of it. Nonetheless, as Faulkner's plot suggests, Isaac's resistance is a resistance to a "natural" process of inextricable racial ambiguity. In *Death Comes for the Archbishop*, the dream of universalism is protested against by pockets of individuated resistance, despite strong efforts to extinguish them from the landscape. Ultimately, Latour's long view, like Isaac's, makes him complicit in the forces he opposes, even if his faith assures their passing. Both novels, then, may be read as anguished and searching examinations of multicultural and multiracial nationalism, where the implications of American indifference are cast in the realm of the imaginary, testing the limitations of social existence that we would recognize as true enough in our own world.

America, the multiculturalists argue, is (or should be) the place not where Crevecoeur's "new man" is fashioned but where all the old ways are maintained with equal validity. In the early twentieth century, processes of Americanization were set in place to destroy ethnic roots and to make the children of Irish and Italian and Greek immigrants into standardized Americans who rolled off the public-school assembly line like Ford automobile parts, interchangeably American except for hair and eye color and the peculiarity of last names. Today, multiculturalists seek to revive and restore lost ethnicities to protect historic differences among peoples from an American meltdown. Classic ethnicity, like classic cars, has value. "The politics of difference" has been cast as "the equivalent of an endangered species act for human beings, where the species to be protected are not owls and snail darters, but Arabs, Jews, homosexuals, Chicanos, Italian Americans, and so on" (Fish 382). We have a sense that unless we do something to protect distinction, human varieties will become, in the United States, no more than stops on a strip of restaurant chains: Taco Bell, Wai-Wai Chinese take-out, Tokyo Today, and Luigi's Italian kitchen—all sites of consumption. But difference in the United States resides, not in essence, but in spectacle, as marketable product, and ultimately as nostalgia.

Multiculturalism is the most recent expression of American romanticism, a perpetual nostalgia for the way we were—or the way someone was—before America, before politics. The role of the endangered species has been taken by a number of players in American history: the noble savage, the happy slave, the angelic child, the immigrant's ethnicity, and, today, that which distinguishes me, that which makes me different. Multiculturalism is a nostalgic impulse, an attempt to freeze time and reverse the leveling of ethnic, religious, and ideological difference that forms the very basis of the United States' challenge to the world. Even the voices of nonconformity in the literary tradition of the United States enforce a paradoxical uniformity. "Whoso would be a man must be a nonconformist" comes from the voice of Ralph Waldo Emerson in "Self-Reliance" (265). "Why should not we have an original relation to the universe?" he asks in "Nature" (190). How can *we all* be nonconformists, how can we all enjoy an original relation to the universe, unless we all, at some point, shed some prior, "unoriginal" quality that defines us? A nation of nonconformists is one in which each makes some private rebellion, by which an allegiance is lost, and then lamented. Recall the grounds on which Ishmael is ultimately seduced by Queequeg in *Moby-Dick*: "I began to be sensible of strange feelings," Ishmael reports. "I felt a melting in me. No more my splintered heart and maddened hand were turned against the wolfish world. The savage had redeemed me. There he sat, his very indifference speaking a nature in which there lurked no civilized hypocrisies and bland deceits" (57). Indifference, in Queequeg, makes the seduction possible and admits Ishmael into his affections.

Isaac McCaslin is a planter; Jean Latour is a missionary. The United States may be considered, historically, as the crossing of (and at times the clash between) values dear to planters and to missionaries. Evoked by Isaac McCaslin and the McCaslin-Beauchamp family is the tradition of planting oneself, as the Puritans said—planting oneself and one's family in a new land in order to establish a new world. The errand into the wilderness, from the city on a hill to the homesteading journey and the resettlement project, is invoked by the image of Lucius Quintus Carothers McCaslin arriving in Mississippi to begin his own agricultural and labor experiment. He came and he stayed put, and generations after him forged ties to the land as strong as any around the world. Isaac McCaslin is thus described on the first page of *Go Down, Moses* as "the inheritor" who, by his own choice, would become "the bequestor" of that property which he permits to pass into his cousin's family. Though he repudiates his inheritance and dissociates himself from the historical significance of *McCaslin*, Isaac does not leave. He disavows his heritage but not his roots, which remain in the very soil of his relinquished property. *Go Down, Moses* ends with the return of another man—or, specifically, of the man's body—a black man who attempted to leave and failed and is brought home so his body may be returned to the land. "He must come home" is the law evoked by the town's attorney, who executes and enforces the edict he unilaterally declares (358). These are the American planters. The hold upon them wielded by the land over which they have sweated and died is cable-strong, as are the ties between the races themselves, denied though they may be by entrenched social convention. Lucas Beauchamp, to whom the McCaslin land should have gone if common law were more powerful than racial antipathy, is described quite simply: "he didn't leave" (106). A life transplanted will cling to its adopted soil, determined to never move again.

And then there are the missionaries. Father Latour reminds us that Americans do much more than plant themselves and prosper; they seek to transform the world into their image and spread their faith in the mutable, transcendent nature of human identity. The history of national and cultural mutation in the United States stands as an affront to sustained ethnicity, producing a reactionary sense of lost identity—or a nostalgia, as I have termed it—and a longing for multiculture rather than conformity to the corporate, industrious, and seemingly solitary loneliness of nuclear America. In the United States, according to the missionary tradition, all things are possible. The missionary takes to heart Emerson's admonition "to look at the world with new eyes" (227) and consider no aspect of human existence immutable. Missionaries neither inherit nor bequest; they establish, they build, and they recruit others to that cause which animates their spirits. "Ah well," explains Latour's close friend and colleague Joseph Vaillant, "that is a missionary's life; to plant where another shall reap" (39). Isaac is inspired and consumed by what has occurred on the land; he is surrounded and nearly *drowned himself* in the commissary, reading the family ledgers. Father Latour is equally inspired by what his faith and vision might bring to pass, by the souls he may convert, and by the future he may affect. As he explains to Latour, "the Cathedral is not for us. . . . We build for the future" (241).

In the opening narrative of *Go Down, Moses*, a card game is played to settle a property dispute, and a slave with much at stake in the game manages to place himself in the role of dealer. "Who dealt these cards?" asks one of the cardplayers, the one who will lose the hand (28). Current generations of Americans are asked to emphasize aspects of their identities that previous generations were expected to hold fast; they play cards in their hands that their parents and grandparents would not have placed on the table. The politics of multiculturalism, to finish the analogy, has much to do with deciding which cards can be played and which cannot. Isaac was born a white landed-inheritor in northern Mississippi in 1867, the son of slave owners. He was to inherit the large plantation established by his grandfather and owned by his father and his uncle. However, Isaac chooses to repudiate his inheritance and to escape its legacy. He is able to accomplish this act—an act he admits is "heresy" to his race, his family, and his cultural inheritance— because, in his own words, "Sam Fathers set me free" (286). Sam Fathers, the Indian hunter, marked Isaac "with something Sam had had in his turn of his vanished and forgotten people" (175), including the refusal to consider land as property. Thus Isaac attempts to accomplish a prototypically American move: trumping one previous affinity—usually a birthright—with another. The move also informs Cather's fiction; it makes Father Latour's missionary journey possible. When the cardinals at Rome discuss who should be elevated to the office of archbishop of the new American territory, they agree that "it would be a grave misfortune if a native priest were appointed" (8) and that someone from elsewhere would be more likely to hold the cards, as it were, for a renewed sense of order and vigor.

The planter Isaac McCaslin and the missionary Jean Latour exist within what we would call today "multicultural" environments, except that there is no assumption of equality among diverse elements. Latour encounters Mexicans, U.S. settlers, and Native Americans, and is himself a Frenchman whose last job was in Cincinnati. Isaac's environment is no less diverse, including whites, blacks, peoples of mixed race, town and country people, and Native Americans. While both men attempt to transcend their nativity, they do so from very different starting points. Nonetheless, each man believes he will be judged more by what he does than what he is and that identity flows from action, or performance, and not from essence. Isaac is "set free" because of what he decides to do with his inheritance—much to the astonishment of himself and others. Father Latour dies a glorious death because of the vast distance he had moved from his origins as a French priest to his end as an American archbishop and because of the cathedral he had built. The question that arises, then, is whether identity in a multicultural environment is performative—the building of a church, the repudiation of an inheritance—or a birthright—the whiteness of McCaslin, the Frenchness of Latour. After all, only the white landowner can relinquish; only the French priest with orders from Rome can bring the universal church to America.

Other characters do not possess the same degree of maneuverability. Lucas Beauchamp, for example, in *Go Down, Moses*, the closest male descendant to Lucius Quintus Carothers McCaslin, does not *choose* to be disinherited because he is counted as a Negro. If he could choose, as Isaac did, he might choose inheritance after all. Lucas is a strong-willed figure described as being "impervious to that blood" which crosses white and black in his body: "[H]e was a vessel, durable, ancestryless, nonconductive, in which the toxin and its anti stalemated one another, seetheless, unrumored in the outside air" (101). However, in the "outside air" of his time and place in America there is nothing Lucas can do to escape or repudiate his social identification as a Negro working on Roth Edmonds's farm. He may be known by Roth to be a descendant of Old Carothers, a "better man" than any Edmonds (112) and *"more like Old Carothers than the rest of us put together"* (114), but none of these known facts changes his essential, racial identity in the eyes of all who see. The freedom that Roth, Isaac, and Latour possess is the freedom to invent themselves, the freedom from predefinition. Lucas comes close, but his social performances are checked. Faulkner says that Lucas *"fathered himself"* and is nearly raceless, but not quite. Multiculturalism creates two classes: those who may perform their lineage and their affinity and those who may not.

As American society presses all peoples within its borders toward conformity, it values highest those activities which are public and observable and devalues those which are not. The Negro graveyard in *Go Down, Moses* contains markers "of a profound meaning and fatal to touch, which no white man could have read" (132). Similarly, Archbishop Latour visits a mountainside "repository of Indian secrets," including those most sacred which "no white man will ever see" (151). That which is inscrutable, which cannot be observed and assessed, threatens the only cohesiveness possible, cohesion established in the public, performative realm of politics. Build a cathedral or repudiate an identity: judgment hinges on what is done and what is said about it. Secret identities, privacy—something Cather certainly knew a lot about—threaten the very order by which we remain universally indifferent to such matters. "The inscrutable thing is chiefly what I hate," says Ahab about the white whale (178). Secrecy fosters divisions that cannot be transcended, and so secrets must be made public, and thus destroyed. As a result, secrets—like trump cards—are guarded with care, lest they threaten outwardly cohesive identities and invite the wrath of the tolerant. Multiculturalism is a parade, not a fatality.

Formalistically, the two novels struggle with cohesion. What Cather says about the mesa plain, that it "had an appearance of great antiquity, and of incompleteness," might be said about her novel. Although never confused with a short-story collection, as *Go Down, Moses* had, Cather's text is equally episodic, to the point where a number of its pieces could be excised from the text as short stories. What is true of Father Valliant, however, is true of both novels: "The man was much greater than the sum of his qualities" (227). In *Death Comes for the Archbishop* and *Go Down, Moses*, Cather and Faulkner, by their distinct gifts, struggle with the very idea of cohesion— thematically, structurally, and aesthetically. Each novel presents a succession of interlocked narratives, and both novels take the long view of a process that no one lives long enough to comprehend entirely, though Latour and Isaac make an approach. And both novels, despite their disjointed structure, possess what we might call a nostalgia for wholeness and cohesion. As a result, they mourn precisely what they are headed toward, despite the resistance encountered in the name of preserving ancient traditions and old ways. It is a point where desire and memory intersect, the essential nature, perhaps, of universalism—either Catholic, in Latour's consciousness, or ontological, in Isaac's.

Recall that the political struggle between Isaac McCaslin and his cousin Cass Edmonds centers on Edmonds's denial of Isaac's freedom and of the entire individualistic enterprise on which Isaac bases his refusal to accept his inheritance. Neither Isaac nor anyone else is "free," Edmonds argues, if freedom means repudiating nativity: "No, not now nor ever, we from them nor they from us," Edmonds asserts. "I am what I am; I will be always what I was born and have always been" (287). Edmond's response to the Adamic impulse in America is present also in Cather's novel, apparent in Latour's lament that "The Mexicans were always Mexicans, the Indians were always Indians." In *Go Down, Moses*, Edmonds, the man who advocates essentialism, suffers a sense of tragic loss for it; in *Death Comes for the Archbishop*, the essentialist is a missionary priest. Nonetheless, each novel continues the politicization of ethnic and racial identity that is at the core of American civilization. In the American Southwest in the mid–nineteenth century, Father Latour does not even know "the extent of this diocese, or this territory" (40); it is a "country . . . still waiting to be made into a landscape" (95). At this point of origins Cather casts her narrative of universality, evoking the dream of America as refuge, where all things are possible. In the American South of the 1940s, it seemed that very few things were possible and that the slate could never be wiped clean—that men acquired aspects of their identities neither "participated in or even seen" (3) but inherited, bequeathed, and descended. Within this context of confinement, characters struggle, like Lucas Beauchamp, for a chance to participate in that original American promise of renegotiated nativity. Isaac fumbles his way toward the same with poignancy, "because I have got myself to have to live with for the rest of my life," he says (275); and although he ultimately fails, his failure has become paradigmatic in the American literary tradition. Isaac is the Ahab of multiculturalism, looking for something to kill— a bear, a grandfather, a legacy—in order to set himself free. His nostalgia leads him to repudiate all that is inscrutable in the land that is secretly his. Why? "It was because there was exactly enough of it. He seemed to see the two of them—himself and the wilderness—as coevals . . . the two spans running out together" (337) leaving him nostalgic well in advance of—but in time to repudiate—any loss.

Nevertheless, divisions of identity—divisions within Americans them- selves, as citizens and as immigrants—are born of the unreconciled dilemma regarding origins. What happens to a shed self? Should it be allowed to wither away like dissolved political bands, or should it be protected, like an endangered species, for future use? Should it be preserved somewhere for the entertainment of those willing to come by and put their dollars down? The answer depends on whether you are running a plantation or building a cathedral. Just as the stability some Americans long for produces a nostalgia for a nation that never existed, multiculturalism is rooted in a nostalgia for an experience that is passing away within the politics of indifference. We can chart an evolution in social policy from permitting the survival of subcultures to the recognition that such survival is a legitimate end in public policy. One may wonder whether in the currency of American culture today, our sights are set on the stability of efficient plantations, or, in Cather's words, on building something "with a purpose so strong that it was like action" (269).

A sure sign that Isaac's beloved wilderness, inhabited by "men, not white nor black nor red but men, hunters" (184), would be spoiled by new structures of identity is the appearance of the locomotive, the paradigmatic machine in the garden. Isaac watches the engine vanish "into the wilderness, dragging its length of train behind it so that it resembled a small dingy harmless snake vanishing into the weeds, drawing him with it too" (304). The train signals a new industrial era when men—black, white, and red—would not be hunters but workers with wagered identities. Archbishop Latour is not troubled by the locomotive on his landscape; its sound, mingled with the church bells from his cathedral, "always amused him here" because it told him, by its whistle, that "He had accomplished an historic period" (271). Cather's novel ends with Latour's sense of cohesion: he becomes a planter; he trades calendared time for eternities. Nonetheless, the last chapter, "Death Comes for the Archbishop," Latour's nominative death warrant, contains narratives of incohesion: "incongruous American building" projects (268), "great industrial expansion" marked by "ruinous reverses" (284); failed genocidal wars to remove the Navajo and Apache tribes (290), and then relocation onto reservations. These matters threaten the vision possessed by Latour in which all his experiences lay "within reach of his hand, and all comprehensible" (288). Isaac is absent from the final pages of *Go Down, Moses*. In the last chapter, also named "Go Down, Moses" and thus (as in Cather's novel) gesturing toward conclusiveness if not cohesion, the town lawyer strong-arms local white businessmen to pay for the return of one of their black sons, recently executed by the state of Illinois. On the face of it, the town has acted cohesively to bury one of its own. However, when the lawyer attends the funeral he is physically repulsed by the extent of the difference he senses between himself and the multiracial, female mourners. The scene echoes Father Latour's experience with Jacinto at Stone Lips, where Latour is "struck by a reluctance, an extreme distaste for the place" (127). "*Soon I will be outside,*" Faulkner's lawyer thinks, "*Then there will be air, space, breath*" (362).

Neither *Go Down, Moses* nor *Death Comes for the Archbishop* has enough air, space, breath, or pages to cohere, finally. Formally, each text is indifferent to the kind of unity one would expect from a culture untroubled by the implications of its legacy. To read these novels one must keep in mind the admonition of Father Martinez: "I advise you to study our native traditions before you begin your reforms," he tells Latour (147). Multiculturalism, I have argued, is the product of a universal nostalgia for nativity. Within the civilization that has repudiated the very concept of ethnicity, a corporate universalism eventually presses indifference upon all who root themselves in it long enough. We have no secrets here. The locomotive is winding its way into the wilderness of Americanization, entangling the sound of its whistle with the bells of the universal church. Latour is confident: this is the landscape of miracles. The United States is a nation of Isaac McCaslins, repudiating the ledgers that account for nativity and preparing, like Jean Latour, to transcend even the most immutable of private anguish and memory in the name of what we must build to accommodate our arrival on the scene. American nostalgia flows readily for lost cultures, lost selves, and discarded identities—the baggage left at terminal points as one explores the metaphysical landscapes of United States.

David Harrell

Afterword

From *The Professor's House* to the Roundhouse—and Beyond

When John N. Swift first contacted me about a Willa Cather symposium he was planning to organize at Mesa Verde National Park, I felt that I was hearing a voice from the past: a very pleasant voice from a very pleasant past. The symposium was tentatively scheduled for October 1999, ten years after I had completed the Ph.D. program at the University of New Mexico and written my dissertation, later published as a book, *From Mesa Verde to* The *Professor's House*. Ten years had also passed since I had last been to Mesa Verde and since I had essentially dropped out of sight of the academic world. I was flattered to be remembered at all, much less to be remembered in such high regard that John wanted me to do one of the plenary sessions—the opening one, it turned out. Having done that, and now writing this afterword for the symposium collection that John and Joe Urgo have assembled, I flatter myself by saying that I have had both the first and the last word on "Willa Cather at Mesa Verde."

Once I realized that John was serious, I began to wonder what I could possibly say that would be of interest to Cather readers and scholars, since I had done no research and no writing to speak of during those ten years. Nor had I made any attempt to keep up with what I was sure was a decade of fine work on *The Professor's House* in particular. A lot can happen—and a lot go unnoticed—in ten years, I realized.

To put my dilemma in perspective: I had enrolled in the Ph.D. program at the University of New Mexico in 1984, the year George Orwell had made sound so ominous and so remotely futuristic. His *1984* notwithstanding, during my entire course of study I used a literal card catalog in the university library, I thought journals indexed on microfiche were the height of miniaturization technology, and I joined others in marveling at the novelty of comments from an outside reader arriving by fax the day before a friend's dissertation defense. I had left this technology—and academic life—behind a decade ago. Then, out of the Mesa Verde blue, John wrote to me via e-mail.

Had I still been in the profession (as I was during the 1970s and early 1980s), I would have tried to prepare something for the symposium about Cather's 1915 visit to Mesa Verde, something on the order of Ann Mosely's narrative accompanied by slides about Cather's Walnut Canyon experience. Or I would have tried to pursue an intriguing hunch about one of Cather's southwestern contacts, as Philip Gerber did. Unable to offer anything like that, however, I realized that all I could do is tell the story of what had happened to me in the last ten years and try, however desperately, to give it an academic or literary slant.

Preparing for the symposium, I felt somewhat like Tom Outland or Roddy Blake poking gingerly among the ruins of another time and place, although the relics I was uncovering were ones I had left behind. Once I returned to the site, I more fully understood Tom's reaction upon returning from Washington: "Once again I had that glorious feeling of being on the mesa, in a world above the world." When combined with my reunion among the true community of Cather scholars, the experience was almost too good to be true—"happiness unalloyed," to use another of Tom's phrases.

The story I told to the symposium participants began with simple dumb luck, and, begging your indulgence, I will retell a little of it here. I read *The Professor's House* for the first time in 1985 in a class in twentieth-century American literature. One day the professor, Bob Fleming, casually remarked that, although it was commonly accepted and believed, contact between the Wetherill family in Mancos, Colorado, and officials at the Smithsonian Institution about the family's discoveries at Mesa Verde had never been actually documented. Two Wetherill authorities—Frank McNitt, Richard's biographer, and later Maurine Fletcher, who edited Al's autobiography—had tried to locate the correspondence but had failed. Acting on the philosophy of "nothing ventured, nothing gained," I sent a letter to the National Anthropological Archives (at that time an investment of twenty-two cents, I believe). Shortly afterward I was astonished to receive not only a very gracious reply from James R. Glenn, deputy director of the archives, but also a copy of a letter from B. K. Wetherill, the father of Richard, Al, John, Clayton, and Winslow, addressed to "Superintendent, Smithsonian Institute." I still remember my excitement at this discovery: the apocryphal correspondence had suddenly become real. (At the symposium, I shared in Matthias Schubnell's excitement over a similar discovery: proof that a German collector had purchased Mesa Verde artifacts from Richard Wetherill at the Chicago World's Fair.)

Shortly afterward, two other letters from Mr. Glenn arrived along with copies of six other pieces of historical correspondence: three more from B. K. Wetherill; two from the secretary of the Smithsonian, Samuel Pierpont Langley; and one from William Henry Holmes, staff archaeologist. Mr. Glenn's explanation for his having found these letters when others had failed was that the archives was better able to locate things during the 1980s than when McNitt and Fletcher had inquired. With this correspondence, I had first-rate material for a paper in the class and sufficient encouragement, particularly from Professor Jim Barbour (who would direct my dissertation) and Professor Paul Andrew Hutton (an outside reader), for on-site research at Mesa Verde. The paper grew into an article for the *New Mexico Historical Review*, the research produced other papers, and all those elements combined into a dissertation and later a book.

But dumb luck could take me only so far. Once I graduated, I spent an entire calendar year looking for work—almost any work, though Tom Outland discouraged me from waiting tables—in or near Santa Fe. Not only was I "unemployed" for the first time in my life, but I was also away from the school setting for the first time in my life: from first grade through my forty-first year I had been on one side of the teacher's desk or the other. Suddenly, I found myself in a world outside the world, having left behind my own Kingdom of Art, my world of glittering ideas, having become a kind of outlander or orphan myself.

Finally, in December 1990, I found a position with the office of the New Mexico secretary of state, Stephanie Gonzales, first as an editor and administrative assistant and finally as director of the newly created Office of Ethics Administration. Thus I made a "dangerous crossing" into the world of state government and politics to occupy a cubicle in the state capitol, a circular four-story structure known as "The Roundhouse."

In 1997 I left what I had thought to be the very epicenter of New Mexico politics and moved into something even more political—public education. I became an analyst for the Legislative Education Study Committee, a bipartisan, bicameral body that reviews and makes recommendations regarding state law and policies for K–12 public education. If, as one newspaper reporter said, I had once been the ethics cop, I was now cast in the role of hired gun, trying not only to keep legislators informed but also to make them look good, especially in their dealings with the governor.

In all my work with state government, I have done my best not only to perform the duties as assigned but also to enhance that performance with the traits and trappings of my background in academics—in other words, instead of merely making the pot functional, I tried to decorate it as well. In this regard, I have found that Willa Cather comes in quite handy. For example, when the secretary of state was asked to write an introductory letter to a book chronicling the WPA artworks in New Mexico, I included in the draft a reference to the "long chain of human endeavor" that Thea Kronborg recognizes in *The Song of the Lark*. When a state representative from Albuquerque was invited to write an op-ed piece in response to some criticism of the public school funding formula, I began the draft with an allusion to the dispute between Tom and Roddy, which ends with Roddy's rueful observation that everything comes to money in the end. Finally, when working during the evenings and on weekends, I have taken a kind of grim, ironic comfort in Roddy's belief that one who has an education will never have to work hard again.

Except for its attempt at a philosophical conclusion, this is where my Mesa Verde story ended, with my becoming a kind of poster child for alternative employment. Then it was my turn to listen to the stories of others, to satisfy my curiosity about the scholarship of the last decade. Many of these stories are retold in the essays in this collection, but the constraints of publication prohibit including all of them. Even so, the range is notable, from the traditional to the experimental, from the personal to the objective. If you have read these pieces, you doubtless share my gratification; if you have not, I commend them to your inspection.

I like to imagine—with some envy—the authors of these stories having returned to their respective academic mesas replete with "glittering ideas." Yet I take a certain satisfaction in what I have learned through my academic background applied to the workaday world of New Mexico state government: that one need not be an artist or an academician to recognize or participate in the creative impulse that Cather recognized as the design of life. Whatever material we carve or tools we use, we are all part of something larger than ourselves, something that started long before we were born and that will continue long after we are gone—something that transcends time—whether it is the traditions of a university, the ever-growing body of knowledge, the work of a state legislature, or even a literary symposium that, given its date and locale, nearly spanned a millennium which—at this writing—is already behind us.

On the last day of the symposium, the plenary speakers were asked to offer some final observations (John, rightfully, had the last word here). For me, the most fitting epigraph came from the story told by the park ranger who took us through Cliff Palace. Archaeologists, he said dramatically, have recently determined that Cliff Palace actually contains far fewer rooms than originally believed. Amazing. Yet the structure itself, of course, is unchanged. It has merely been reconfigured, redefined, reinterpreted. Like a literary text, it used to mean one thing; now it means another. But there is more. The ranger's story also raised a question about the text's authenticity: some of the vigas, or beams, presumed to have been part of the original construction centuries ago were discovered through an inventory of park records to have been added in the early twentieth century. What was thought old is really new, what was thought fixed is really mutable.

What the ranger's account suggests to me is that Cather's work, like Cliff Palace, can accommodate—or withstand—whatever critics and scholars subject it to. As demonstrated by the papers presented at the symposium, Cather's work is so rich that it lends itself to explication from multiple directions through multiple disciplines: not only literary analysis but also history, biography, geography, archaeology, linguistics, and psychology, and even personal reflection. Moreover, Cather's writings can accommodate these various readings for as long as the design of life plays out in human endeavor. Sometimes, whether through choice or circumstance, we must let go of some things with the hand and others with the mind, but the design of life continues as long as we never let go with the heart. Mine, it seems, is not the last word after all.

Works Cited

Adams, Henry. *Novels, Mont Saint Michel, The Education*. Ed. Ernest and Jayne N. Samuels. New York: Library of America, 1983.

Ammons, Elizabeth. *Conflicting Stories: American Women Writers at the Turn into the Twentieth Century*. New York: Oxford University Press, 1991.

Anaya Rudolfo. *Bless Me, Ultima*. 1972. New York: Warner Books, 1999.

Anderson Imbert, Enrique. "Literatura fantástica, realismo mágico, y lo real maravilloso." *Otros Mundos, Otros Fuegos: Fantasía y Realismo Mágico en Iberoamérica*. Ed. Donald A Yates. Lansing: Michigan State University Press, 1975. 39–45.

———. *El realismo mágico y otros ensayos*. Caracas: Monte Avila, 1976.

Austin, Mary. *Earth Horizon*. 1932. Albuquerque: University of New Mexico Press, 1991.

———. *The Land of Journeys' Ending*. New York: Century, 1924.

Bederman, Gail. *Manliness and Civilization: A Cultural History of Gender and Race in the United States, 1880–1917*. Chicago: University of Chicago Press, 1995.

Berlant, Lauren. *The Queen of America Goes to Washington City: Essays on Sex and Citizenship*. Durham: Duke University Press, 1997.

Berlo, Janet Catherine, ed. *The Early Years of Native American Art History*. Seattle: University of Washington Press, 1992.

Boyd, Elizabeth. *Popular Arts of Spanish New Mexico*. Santa Fe: Museum of New Mexico Press, 1974.

Brooks, Cleanth, R. W. B. Lewis, and Robert Penn Warren, eds. *American Literature: The Makers and the Making*, Book C (1861–1914). New York: St. Martin's, 1973.

Buell, Lawrence. *The Environmental Imagination: Thoreau, Nature Writing, and the Formation of American Culture*. Cambridge: Harvard University Press, 1995.

Butler, Judith. *Bodies That Matter: On the Discursive Limits of Sex*. New York: Routledge, 1993.

Calderón, Héctor. "Rudolfo Anaya's *Bless Me, Ultima*: A Chicano Romance of the Southwest." *Crítica* 1.3 (1986): 21–47

Callander, Marilyn B. *Willa Cather and the Fairy Tale*. Ann Arbor, Mich.: UMI, 1989.

Cantú, Roberto. "Review of *Bless Me, Ultima*." *Mester* 4.1 (1973): 66–68.

Cash, Marie Romero. *Santos: Enduring Images of Northern New Mexico Village Churches*. Niwot: University Press of Colorado, 1999.

Cather, Willa. *Alexander's Bridge*. 1912. Lincoln: University of Nebraska Press, 1977.

———. *Death Comes for the Archbishop*. 1927. New York: Vintage, 1990.

———. Letter to Paul Reynolds. 26 April 1926. Columbia University Library, New York.

———. *My Ántonia*. Boston: Houghton Mifflin, 1918.

———. *My Mortal Enemy*. 1926. New York: Vintage, 1990.

———. *Not Under Forty*. 1936. Lincoln: University of Nebraska Press, 1988.

———. *One of Ours*. 1922. New York: Vintage, 1991.

———. Preface. *Alexander's Bridge*. Boston: Houghton Mifflin, 1922.

———. *The Professor's House*. 1925. New York: Vintage, 1990.

———. *Shadows on the Rock*. 1931. New York: Vintage, 1995

———. *The Song of the Lark*. 1915; rev. 1937. New York: Houghton Mifflin, 1983.

———. *Willa Cather On Writing: Critical Studies on Writing as an Art*. New York: Knopf, 1949.

Chief Seattle, "Our People Are Ebbing Away Like a Rapidly Receding Tide." *Political Thought in the United States: A Documentary History*. Ed. Lyman Tower Sargent. New York: New York University Press, 1997. 227–29.

Clark, John R. *The Modern Satiric Grotesque and Its Traditions*. Lexington: University Press of Kentucky, 1991.

Clifford, James. "Introduction: Partial Truths." *Writing Culture: The Poetics and Politics of Ethnography*. Ed. James Clifford and George E. Marcus. Berkeley: University of California Press, 1986. 1–26.

———. "On Ethnographic Allegory." *Writing Culture: The Poetics and Politics of Ethnography*. Ed. James Clifford and George E. Marcus. Berkeley: University of California Press, 1986. 98–121.

Crevecoeur, J. Hector St. John de. *Letters from an American Farmer and Sketches of Eighteenth-Century America*. New York: Viking Penguin, 1981.

Crow, Charles L. "The Patrimony of Blue Mesa: *The Professor's House* and Museum Theory." *Willa Cather Pioneer Memorial Newsletter* 41.3 (1997–98): 53–57.

Crowley, John W. *The Dean of American Letters: The Late Career of William Dean Howells*. Amherst: University of Massachusetts Press, 1999.

Curtin, William, ed. *The World and the Parish: Willa Cather's Articles and Reviews, 1893–1902*. 2 vols. Lincoln: University of Nebraska Press, 1970.

Danow, David K. *The Spirit of Carnival: Magical Realism and the Grotesque*. Lexington: University Press of Kentucky. 1995.

Dennis, Helen M. "Tonight Mrs. Forrester Began 'Once upon a Time': Origins and Traces in the Work of Willa Cather." *Willa Cather and European Cultural Influences*. Ed. H. M. Dennis Lewiston. New York: Edwin Mellon, 1996. 33–52.

DeVoto, Bernard. *Letters from the Earth: Uncensored Writings of Mark Twain*. New York: Harper and Row, 1962.

DiNunzio, Mario R., ed. *Theodore Roosevelt: An American Mind—A Selection from His Writings*. New York: Penguin, 1994.

Dipple, Brian W. *Catlin and His Contemporaries: The Politics of Patronage*. Lincoln: University of Nebraska Press, 1990.

Emerson, Ralph Waldo. *Selected Writings of Ralph Waldo Emerson*. New York: Signet, 1983.

Faulkner, William. *Go Down, Moses*. 1942. New York: Vintage International, 1990.

Feld, Rose C. "Restlessness Such as Ours Does Not Make for Beauty: In an Interview Miss Willa S. Cather Discusses America and Its Literature." *New York Times Book Review* 24 December 1924: 11.

Fewkes, Jesse Walter. *Antiquities of the Mesa Verde National Park: Cliff Palace*. Bureau of American Ethnology. Bulletin 51. Washington DC: Government Printing Office, 1911.

Fish, Stanley. "Boutique Multiculturalism, or Why Liberals Are Incapable of Thinking about Hate Speech." *Critical Inquiry* 23.2 (1997): 378–95.

Frank, Larry. *New Kingdom of the Saints: Religious Art of New Mexico, 1780–1907*. Santa Fe: Red Crane Books, 1992.

Frost, Robert. *Complete Poems of Robert Frost*. New York: Holt, 1949.

Gerber, Philip. *Willa Cather*. Boston: Twayne, 1975.

Goldberg, Jonathan. "Strange Brothers." *Novel Gazing: Queer Readings in Fiction*. Ed. Eve Kosofsky Sedgwick. Durham: Duke University Press, 1997. 465–82.

Green, Constance McLaughlin. *Washington: Capital City, 1879–1950*. Princeton: Princeton University Press, 1963.

Haller, Evelyn. "*Death Comes for the Archbishop*: A Map of Intersecting Worlds." *Willa Cather Pioneer Memorial Newsletter* 34.3 (1990): 15–21.

Harbison, Sherrill. Introduction. *The Song of the Lark*. By Willa Cather. New York: Penguin, 1999. vii–xxxi.

Harrell, David. *From Mesa Verde to* The Professor's House. Albuquerque: University of New Mexico Press, 1992.

————. "'We contacted Smithsonian': The Wetherills at Mesa Verde." *New Mexico Historical Review* 63 (July 1987): 229–48.

Hawthorne, Nathaniel. *The Scarlet Letter*. 1850. New York: Norton, 1978

Hinsley, Curtis M., Jr. *Savages and Scientists: The Smithsonian Institution and the Development of American Anthropology 1846- 1910*. Washington DC: Smithsonian Institution Press, 1981.

Hively, Evelyn H. *Sacred Fire: Willa Cather's Novel Cycle*. Lanham MD: University Press of America, 1994.

Hughes, J. Donald. *American Indian Ecology*. El Paso: Texas Western Press, 1987.

Irigaray, Luce. "The Blind Spot of an Old Dream of Symmetry." *Speculum of the Other Woman*. Trans. Gillian Gill. Ithaca: Cornell University Press, 1985

Kates, George N., ed. "Willa Cather's Unfinished Avignon Story." *Willa Cather Collected Stories*. New York: Vintage, 1992. 464–93.

Keeler, Clinton. "Narrative without Accent: Willa Cather and Puvis de Chavannes." *American Quarterly* 17 (1965): 119–26.

Krech, Shephard, III. *The Ecological Indian: Myth and History*. New York: Norton, 1999.

Krickeberg, Walter. *Ältere Ethnographica aus Nordamerika im Berliner Museum für Völkerkunde*. Baessler-Archiv Beiträge zur Voelkerkunde. Neue Folge Band II. Berlin: Verlag von Dietrich Reimer, 1954.

Krieger, K., and G. Koch, eds. *100 Jahre Museum Fuer Voelkerkunde Berlin*. Baessler-Archiv Beiträge zur Völkerkunde. Neue Folge Band XXI. Berlin: Verlag von Dietrich Reimer, 1973.

Kristeva, Julia. "Black Sun." 1987. *The Portable Kristeva*. Ed. Kelly Oliver. New York: Columbia University Press, 1997. 180–202.

Lee, Hermione. *Willa Cather: Double Lives*. New York: Pantheon, 1990.

Lee, Ronald F. *The Antiquities Act of 1906*. Washington DC: National Park Service, U.S. Department of the Interior, 1970.

Lewis, Edith. *Willa Cather Living*. New York: Knopf, 1953.

Lindemann, Marilee. *Willa Cather: Queering America*. New York: Columbia University Press, 1999.

Lloyd, Jill. *German Expressionism: Primitivism and Modernity*. New Haven: Yale University Press, 1991.

Love, Glen A. "*The Professor's House*: Cather, Hemingway, and the Chastening of American Prose Style." *Western American Literature* 24.4 (1990): 295–311.

Luhan, Mabel Dodge. *Edge of the Taos Desert*. 1937. Albuquerque: University of New Mexico Press, 1987.

Marcus, George E., and Michael M. J. Fischer. *Anthropology as Cultural Critique: An Experimental Moment in the Human Sciences*. Chicago: University of Chicago Press, 1986.

Melville, Herman. *Moby-Dick*. 1851. New York: Penguin, 1992.

Mena, Lucía I. "Fantasía y realismo mágico." *Otros Mundos, Otros Fuegos: Fantasía y Realismo Mágico en Iberoamérica*. Ed. Donald A. Yates. Lansing: Michigan State University Press, 1975. 63–69.

Michaels, Walter Benn. *Our America: Nativism, Modernism, and Pluralism*. Durham: Duke University Press, 1995.

———. "The Vanishing American." *American Literary History* 2.2 (1990): 220–41.

Mosely, Anne. "Cathedral Building in Cather's *My Mortal Enemy*: Myra Henshawe as Spiritual Grotesque." *Literature and Belief* 18.2 (1998): 34–52.

Murphy, John J. "Explanatory Notes." *Death Comes for the Archbishop*. 1927. Willa Cather scholarly ed. Ed. John J. Murphy. Lincoln: University of Nebraska Press, 1999. 381–511.

Museum für Völkerkunde, Erwerbungsakte, vol. 26, Akte 511/05.

Nealon, Christopher. "Affect Genealogy: Feeling and Affiliation in Willa Cather." *American Literature* 69.1 (1997): 5–37.

Nordenskiöld, Gustaf. *The Cliff Dwellers of the Mesa Verde, Southwestern Colorado: Their Pottery and Implements*. 1893. Intro. Watson Smith. Trans. D. Lloyd Morgan. New York: AMS, 1973.

O'Brien, Sharon. Introduction. *The Song of the Lark*. By Willa Cather. New York: Signet-Penguin, 1991. v–xviii.

———, ed. *Stories, Poems and Other Works*. New York: Library of America, 1992.

Pastor Bodmer, Beatriz. *The Armature of Conquest: Spanish Accounts of the Discovery of America, 1492–1549*. Stanford: Stanford University Press, 1992.

Pearce, T. M. *Literary America, 1903–1934: The Mary Austin Letters*. Westport CT: Greenwood, 1979.

Preston, Douglas. "Cannibals of the Canyon." *New Yorker* 30 November 1998: 76–89.

Quirk, Tom, ed. *Mark Twain: Tales, Speeches, Essays, and Sketches*. New York: Penguin, 1994.

———. *Coming to Grips with "Huckleberry Finn": Essays on a Book, a Boy, and a Man*. Columbia: University of Missouri Press, 1993.

Reader's Digest. *Our Native American Heritage*. Pleasantville NY: Reader's Digest, 1996.

Rogers, Jane. "The Function of the Llorona Motif in Anaya's *Bless Me, Ultima*." *Contemporary Chicano Fiction: A Critical Survey*. Ed. Vernon E. Lattin. Binghamton: Bilingual, 1986. 200–205.

Romero, Lora. *Home Fronts: Domesticity and Its Critics in the Antebellum United States*. Durham: Duke University Press, 1997.

Rosaldo, Renato. *Culture and Truth: The Remaking of Social Analysis*. Boston: Beacon, 1989.

Rothman, Hal. *Preserving Different Pasts: The American National Monuments*. Urbana: University of Illinois Press, 1989.

Rudnick, Lois Palken. *Mabel Dodge Luhan: New Woman, New Worlds*. Albuquerque: University of New Mexico Press, 1984.

———. *Utopian Vistas: The Mabel Dodge Luhan House and the American Counterculture*. Albuquerque: University of New Mexico Press, 1996.

Rydell, Robert W. *All the World's a Fair: Visions of Empire at American International Expositions, 1876–1916*. Chicago: University of Chicago Press, 1984.

Saldivar, José D. "Postmodern Realism." Ed. Emory Elliott.*Columbia Literary History of the American Novel*. New York: Columbia University Press, 1991. 521–41.

Saldívar, Ramón. *Chicano Narrative: The Dialectics of Difference*. Madison: University of Wisconsin Press, 1990.

Sanner, Hans-Ulrich. E-mail message to Matthias Schubnell, 23 September 1999.

Schwind, Jean. "This Is a Frame-Up." *Cather Studies* 2. Lincoln: University of Nebraska Press, 1993.

Sedgwick, Eve Kosofsky. *Tendencies*. Durham: Duke University Press, 1993.

Sergeant, Elizabeth Shepley, *Willa Cather: A Memoir*. New York: J. B. Lippincott, 1953.

Silko, Leslie Marmon. "An Old-Time Indian Attack Conducted in Two Parts." *This Remembered Earth: An Anthology of Contemporary Native American Literature*. Ed. Geary Hobson. Albuquerque: University of New Mexico Press-Red Earth Press, 1979. 211–16.

Steele, Thomas J. *Santos and Saints: The Religious Folk Art of Hispanic New Mexico*. Santa Fe: Ancient City Press, 1994.

Stocking, George W., Jr. *Race, Culture, and Evolution: Essays in the History of Anthropology*. New York: Free Press-Macmillan, 1968.

Stout, Janis P. "Willa Cather and Mary Austin: Intersections and Influences." *Southwestern American Literature* 21.2 (1996): 39–59.

Swift, John N. "Memory, Myth, and *The Professor's House*." *Western American Literature* 20.4 (1986): 301–14.

Swift, John N., and Tschetter, Ann. "A Nebraska 'Mummy' and a Poem: One Source for Mother Eve." *Willa Cather Pioneer Memorial Newsletter* 43.1 (1999): 14–15.

Synnott, Kevin. "The Color of an Adventure: Pictorial Dimensions in Cather's Archbishop." *Willa Cather Pioneer Memorial Newsletter*31.3 (1987): 11–15.

Thoreau, Henry David. *Walden and Civil Disobedience*. New York: Penguin, 1983

Todorov, Tzevetan. *Introduction à la littérature fantastique*. Paris: Du Seuil, 1970.

Turner, Christy G., II, and Jacqueline A. Turner. *Man Corn: Cannibalism and Violence in the Prehistoric American Southwest*. Salt Lake City: University of Utah Press, 1999.

Twain, Mark. *The Bible According to Mark Twain*. Ed. Howard G. Baetzhold and Joseph B. McCullough. New York: Simon and Schuster, 1996.

———. *Collected Tales, Sketches, Speeches, 1891–1910*. Ed. Louis Budd. Vol. 2. New York: Library of America, 1992.

Ude, Wayne. "Forging an American Style: The Romance-Novel and Magical Realism as Response to the Frontier and Wilderness Experiences." *The Frontier Experience and the American Dream*. Ed. David Mogen. College Station: Texas A & M University Press, 1989. 50–63.

———. "North American Magical Realism." *Colorado State Review* 8.2 (1981): 21–30.

Van Vechten. "To Blanche Knopf." *Letters of Carl Van Vechten*. Ed. Bruce Kellner. New Haven: Yale University Press, 1987. 148.

Walter, Roland. *Magical Realism in Contemporary Chicano Fiction*. Frankfurt am Main: Vervuert Verlag, 1993.

Weigle, Marta. *Brothers of Light, Brothers of Blood: The Penitentes of the Southwest*. Santa Fe: Ancient City Press, 1976.

Wharton, Edith. *The Age of Innocence*. New York: Signet Classic, 1996.

Woodress, James. *Willa Cather: A Literary Life*. Lincoln: University of Nebraska Press, 1987

Wroth, William. *Images of Penance, Images of Mercy: Southwestern* Santos*in the Late Nineteenth Century*. Norman: University of Oklahoma Press, 1991.

Zamora, Lois P. "Magical Romance/Magical Realism: Ghosts in U.S. and Latin American Fiction." *Magical Realism: Theory, History, Community*. Ed. Lois P. Zamora and W. B. Faris. Durham: Duke University Press, 1995. 497–550.

Ziomek, Henry. *Lo grotesco en la literatura española del Siglo de Oro*. Madrid: Alcalá, 1983.

Contributors

Manuel Broncano is Associate Professor of American Literature and Chair of the Department of English at the University of León, Spain. He has edited and translated into Spanish Willa Cather's *Death Comes for the Archbishop* and Flannery O'Connor's *Wise Blood*. He is the author of *Mundos Breves, Mundos Infinitos: Flannery O'Connor y el cuento norteamericano*, the only study of O'Connor's short stories available in Spanish. He is currently engaged in a book-length project on magical realism as an American mode.

Mary Chinery is Assistant Professor of English at Georgian Court College in Lakewood, New Jersey, and has published articles in the *Willa Cather Pioneer Memorial Newsletter* and *Transformations*. She serves on the board of the New Jersey College English Association

Ann Fisher-Wirth is Professor of English at the University of Mississippi, where she teaches American literature, literature and environment, and creative writing. She is the author of *William Carlos Williams and Autobiography: The Woods of His Own Nature* (Pennsylvania State University Press, 1989) and of numerous articles on Willa Cather, William Carlos Williams, Anita Brookner, Louise Glück, Cormac McCarthy, Robert Hass, and other writers. She has published essays on environmental issues, and her poems appear in many national journals.

David Harrell is the author of *From Mesa Verde to* The Professor's House and of essays on Cather's literary relationship to the excavation at Mesa Verde. He received his Ph.D in English in 1989 from the University of New Mexico and has held several positions with the government of the state of New Mexico. He and his family live in Santa Fe.

Marilee Lindemann is Associate Professor and Associate Director of graduate studies in English at the University of Maryland, College Park. She is the author of *Willa Cather: Queering America* (Columbia University Press, 1999) and of essays on Cather, Jewett, and queer studies in American literature. She edited *Alexander's Bridge* (1997) and *O Pioneers!* (1999) for Oxford University Press.

Richard H. Millington is Professor of English at Smith College. He has published essays on *My Ántonia* and *Shadows on the Rock* and is the author of *Practicing Romance: Narrative Form and Cultural Engagement in Hawthorne's Fiction* (Princeton University Press, 1992) as well as of several essays on Hawthorne. He is the coeditor of *Hitchcock's America* (Oxford University Press, 1999), which includes his essay on *North by Northwest*, and he is editing the *Cambridge Companion to Nathaniel Hawthorne*, now in preparation.

John J. Murphy teaches American literature at Brigham Young University, where he edits the journal *Literature and Belief*. He is the author of *My Ántonia: The Road Home* (Twayne, 1989) and of more than sixty essays on Cather in books and scholarly journals. A member of the editorial board for the Cather scholarly edition, he is the volume editor of *Death Comes for the Archbishop* (University of Nebraska Press, 1999) and co–volume editor with David Stouck of *Shadows on the Rock* (University of Nebraska Press, forthcoming). His collections on Cather include *Critical Essays on Willa Cather* (GK Hall, 1984) and *Willa Cather: Family, Community, and History* (Brigham Young University, 1990). He has also published on Hawthorne, Wharton, and Flannery O'Connor.

Tom Quirk is Professor of English at the University of Missouri, Columbia. He is the volume editor for the Cather scholarly edition of *Alexander's Bridge*. His recent books include *Nothing Abstract: Investigations in the American Literary Imagination* (University of Missouri Press, 2000) and *Mark Twain: A Study of the Short Fiction* (Twayne, 1997).

Christopher Schedler received his Ph.D. in English from the University of California, Santa Barbara. His work has appeared in *Texas Studies in*

Literature and Language, *Hemingway Review*, and *Arizona Quarterly*. His essay is adapted from his dissertation, "Modernist Borders of Our America."

Matthias Schubnell is a native of Freiburg, Germany. He holds a Ph.D. from the University of Oxford, where he studied as a Rhodes Scholar. He teaches at the University of the Incarnate Word in San Antonio and has published two books on N. Scott Momaday: a critical biography (University of Oklahoma Press, 1985) and a collection of interviews (University Press of Mississippi, 1996). He has also published articles on Leslie Marmon Silko, Jimmy Santiago Baca, Frank Waters, Momaday, and Willa Cather.

Merrill Maguire Skaggs is a frequent speaker and writer on Willa Cather and the author of *After the World Broke in Two: The Later Novels of Willa Cather* (University Press of Virginia, 1990). She edited and contributed to *Willa Cather's New York: New Essays on Cather and the City* (Fairleigh Dickinson University Press, 2000). Her most recent research interest involves Willa Cather and William James. She teaches in the Caspersen School of Graduate Studies at Drew University.

John N. Swift teaches modern literature and chairs the Department of English and Comparative Literary Studies at Occidental College in Los Angeles. The author of several essays on Cather and her work, he is president of the Willa Cather Pioneer Memorial and Educational Foundation of Red Cloud, Nebraska.

Joseph R. Urgo is Professor and Chair of the Department of English at the University of Mississippi. He is the author of *Willa Cather and the Myth of American Migration* (University of Illinois Press, 1995) and *In the Age of Distraction* (University Press of Mississippi, 2000).

Index